To:

....

From:

....

Date:

....

PRAISE FOR *LOVE HEALS*

I am a great admirer of Becca Stevens and her work and have been fortunate to connect with her in various settings. In her, I see a truly old soul in this incredibly modern package, and any conversation with Becca feels like an invitation to experience history, poetry, nature, God . . . When I'm reading her words, I feel like I'm tapping into this rich, ancient wisdom delivered by someone who I could just as easily spend hours chatting and laughing together with over coffee—or tea in her case!

Love Heals transports me to that chair beside Becca where I am listening to these great but simple truths revealed through her reflections. This book is just an extension of the way that she naturally ponders creation, ponders nature, ponders life and in turn engages us to participate in her journey. Everything and everyone has a purpose, and everything works together in the most amazing community. Even things that are scary have their place in the exquisite order of the world that Becca celebrates. *Love Heals* is true. And in this book I've found a beautiful place of encouragement and hope—a meeting point for us all to experience community, healing, and love.

—AMY GRANT

I love Becca Stevens and love what she has created with Thistle Farms. This inspiring insight into her daily life is so valuable and necessary. Amidst all the noise and chaos of our world, Becca finds God in simple, beautiful, quiet places, and tells us we can too.

—KIMBERLY WILLIAMS-PAISLEY

LOVE HEALS

BECCA STEVENS

THOMAS NELSON
Since 1798

Published in Nashville, Tennessee, by Thomas Nelson. Thomas Nelson is a registered trademark of HarperCollins Christian Publishing, Inc.

Published in association with literary agent Roberta Croteau.

Photos on pages 64 and 132 were taken by Taro Yamasaki. The photo on page 79 was taken by Shravan Vidyarthi. The photo on pages 76 and 77 is care of Hands Producing Hope, Rwanda. Peggy Napier took the remainder of the photos.

The quote "Grant that your love may so fill our lives . . ." from St. Ignatius of Loyola in chapter 4 is taken from Woodeene Koenig-Bricker's *Praying With the Saints* (Chicago: Loyola Press, 2001), 118.

The quote "It is true that this sin is the cause . . ." from Julian of Norwich in chapter 11 is taken from Julian of Norwich, *Revelations of Divine Love*, trans. Elizabeth Spearing (New York: Penguin Books, 1998), 80.

The CBS study on stress mentioned in chapter 13 can be found at the CBS News website, at http://www.cbsnews.com/news/why-stress-kills/.

Thomas Nelson titles may be purchased in bulk for educational, business, fund-raising, or sales promotional use. For information, please e-mail SpecialMarkets@ThomasNelson.com.

Unless otherwise noted, Scripture quotations are taken from the HOLY BIBLE: NEW INTERNATIONAL VERSION®. © 1973, 1978, 1984, 2011 by Biblica, Inc.™ Used by permission of Zondervan. All rights reserved worldwide. www.zondervan.com. The "NIV"and "New International Version" are trademarks registered in the United States Patent and Trademark Office by Biblica, Inc.™

Used by permission of Zondervan Publishing House. All rights reserved.

Scripture quotations marked ESV are taken from the ESV® Bible (The Holy Bible, English Standard Version®). Copyright © 2001 by Crossway, a publishing ministry of Good News Publishers. Used by permission. All rights reserved.

Scripture quotations marked NKJV are taken from the New King James Version®. © 1982 by Thomas Nelson. Used by permission. All rights reserved.

Scripture quotations marked NLT are taken from the *Holy Bible*, New Living Translation. © 1996, 2004, 2007, 2013 by Tyndale House Foundation. Used by permission of Tyndale House Publishers, Inc., Carol Stream, Illinois 60188. All rights reserved.

Scripture quotations marked NRSV are taken from the New Revised Standard Version Bible. copyright © 1989 National Council of the Churches of Christ in the United States of America. Used by permission. All rights reserved.

ISBN-13: 978-0-7180-9455-3

Printed in China

17 18 19 20 /DSC/ 9 8 7 6 5 4 3 2 1

This book is dedicated to Marlei Olson and Hal Cato, who lead with healing grace.

In addition I am grateful for thistle farmers such as Regina, Carlana, Holli, Cary, Shelia, Katrina, Dorris, Tracey, Gwen, Donna, and countless others who have grown this community that allows love to heal.

I am changed by their love.

CONTENTS

CONTENTS

PREFACE

Where It All Began

ove heals has always been the tagline at Thistle Farms, the community I founded more than twenty years ago. Thistle Farms began out of gratitude and hope for all the mercy and healing I'd experienced myself and my realization that, in the end, love is the most powerful force for change in the world.

After I was ordained in 1991 and started working as a chaplain five years later, some friends and I opened the first sanctuary for women survivors of trafficking, addiction, and prostitution. Five pioneers came into that first house, called Magdalene. It changed not only their lives but

mine—dramatically. That community was a powerful witness that acceptance, commitment, and love help women find healing from some of the
oldest and deepest scars this world has ever known. After a couple years
of meeting with survivors and witnessing miracles of healing love, I knew
that I would be doing this work for the rest of my life. The survivor-leaders
were living with a new power and grace that I knew could potentially bring
healing healing throughout the world.

After four years, we realized women had to be economically independent in order to gain control of their destinies. So we started what is known
as a "social enterprise," where the workforce itself is the mission of the
business. We named it Thistle Farms, and we began by manufacturing and
selling all-natural candles and body balm. The line of healing products has
expanded to more than thirty offerings and brings in millions of dollars
in revenue to support the growing mission. Thistle Farms grew from an
initial team of five women to a global enterprise that employs more than
eighteen hundred women survivors via global trade.

We have also helped start more than sixty sister programs throughout
the United States and offer outreach to seven hundred women annually.
About thirty-five women at a time live in the community. Each resident has
two years of free housing that offers sanctuary and also includes job training, medical care, education, therapy, and guidance for spiritual growth.
There is poetic justice in producing healing and nourishing products for
the body, all crafted by women whose bodies have endured years of abuse.

Love is the most powerful force for change in the world.

Through this social enterprise, Thistle Farms residents and graduates find their way back from a world that, through unjust systems and broken families, helped them make their way to the streets. As part of Thistle Farms, women survivors are bankers, manufacturing directors, baristas, distributors, social media marketers, facilitators, case managers, outreach directors, receptionists, candle makers, and paper makers. Many of the leaders at Thistle Farms are just coming into their own as business executives, salespeople, and entrepreneurs. With love as our business model, we are still growing and healing some twenty years later.

Whether we are pouring wax for the candles we light for the next woman finding her way home, sharing fabrics from Indonesia that tell the story of our sisters' journey to financial freedom, or serving a cup of hot thistle tea to a sojourner who visits our Thistle Stop Café, this work is about freedom, sanctuary, love, and healing.

The women of Thistle Farms have taught me countless things about the healing we all need—all the time. The healing we have found at Thistle Farms is not a miracle cure; it's about finding our way to wholeness. Healing can take time and effort, and it is a central part of our entire lives. Our journeys begin and end with God, so this life is a discovery of how love heals us along the way.

I hope you'll join me and the women of Thistle Farms as we take this walk toward healing together.

Our journeys begin
and end with God, so
this life is a discovery
of how love heals
us along the way.

I believe that love heals.

And when I forget

I believe that

I connect to creation,

Commit to a daily practice,

Cultivate compassion,

Create a grateful heart,

And come home to myself.

Then I remember.

INTRODUCTION

Love Heals

*L*ove heals. That simple phrase holds the essence of hope and the deepest truth. I learned this lesson profoundly on one of the worst days of my life.

My mom was in the ICU with an undiagnosed terminal brain disease, and I was having a miscarriage. I felt lost and broken. I wasn't sure what to pray for or who to turn to. A nurse walked into my mom's hospital room and asked if Mom was the wife of Reverend Joe Stevens. He had been dead for almost thirty years, after a drunk driver hit him, and he had served in that community for only one year. I didn't think anyone in Nashville, Tennessee, remembered him. Except, apparently, this woman.

She said that when she was a girl, my father had helped her family through a crisis and that he'd been visiting their house right before he was killed on his way home. She credited him with saving her mom and dad's marriage and then said to me, "I am honored to take care of your mom."

A peace that passes understanding washed over me. *I am not lost; I am found.* The love my father had offered decades before was surrounding my mother and me still. I knew that even in the midst of death and brokenness, love heals.

Love heals is the principle that has shaped the way I have tried to live my life. I have tried to make room for that healing through gratitude, awareness, and acceptance. For example, if I am floating down a river, I don't mind if the current turns me around and I float backward for a bit. It gives me a chance to see where I have been, and I have time to study the trees and the sky. If I am serving at the altar as a pastor, I try to look at the candles, notice the light, and be present to the Holy Spirit in the worship. If I am with my husband and kids, I try to stay off my phone and marvel at the gift of family. Sometimes when the laundry has piled up or I have a work deadline that I'm not sure I'll make, I still try to take a walk in the morning and remember to say my prayers. *Love heals* is as simple as that for me— and still, it is hard to practice.

Everyone could use more healing in their lives. We could all use some space to dream about what healing might look like for us. Healing may mean finding peace after trauma, feeling hope in the midst of grief,

forgiving after being hurt, or just relief from the daily wear and tear of living in a broken world. We can all use a reminder of the good news that love heals. This book is designed first to help you remember how love heals and then to help you be more intentional about practicing and welcoming the healing power of love in the places where you hurt. Each chapter offers a different angle on the healing properties of love. You will find some practical steps you can take, some new practices that might make a difference in your overall healing, some poetry to lift your spirit, and hopefully some new thoughts to carry you to new places. These images and writings are offered to help you look again at ancient ideas and well-worn words with new eyes.

I hope this book is a gift to you. I hope it carries you through grief and beyond shame and that it opens up new roads as you grow and heal. Getting a new perspective on our old issues can open up space for healing. On the path of love, it's not so much what we look at that is important but what we see. Jesus didn't say we have to observe something as majestic as a bald eagle to be inspired; He said to consider again the common sparrow and see how we are loved.

I also hope this book inspires and energizes you to put ancient rituals that carry love's healing into daily practice. For example, using essential oils, drinking a healing cup of herbal tea, and walking in nature are three very simple rituals that can bring more healing into your day. Having a good prayer practice, learning and speaking truth, and transforming brokenness into compassion can help bring healing love to yourself and others.

Read this book, and take away anything that is helpful. Leave the rest, and walk in love as a beloved child of God.

Love Rains Down

Pear blossoms are falling like snow this spring,
Soft petals covering passing pilgrims
like unceasing prayers.
Breathing in fragrant abundance,
I can't remember the cold winter's bare branches.
Pear blossoms in wide-open fields
Preach with grace that all of creation,
from Eden on,
Rains down love.

CHAPTER 1

LOVE HEALS THROUGH CREATION

Recognizing God's love in nature

God's Green Earth

There are days when hillsides blush in tenderness

And moments when valleys are unshadowed.

There are seasons when streams roll with justice

And all creation blooms where it is planted.

There are times when we feel God's pulse

Through lapping waves, clapping trees,

And the woodpecker's happy drumming.

There are mornings when we feel the sunrise

Like warm tea on the backs of our throats.

There are spaces where even weeds

And crawly things call us back to grace.

That is when our hearts sing "Alleluia"

And praise God's green earth.

The story of faith begins with the unfolding of God's love over the earth. Love is written into the very fabric of creation. Throughout Scripture we read about love's healing power, from the first vision of a garden with a tree of life to the last vision of a kingdom where that same tree stood, with leaves that were made for "the healing of the nations" (Revelation 22:2). Today we can imagine the roots of that tree running under our feet, calling us to remember God's healing power all around us and in us.

We are part of God's creation. We have saltwater like the ocean for tears, dirt in our DNA, and the same matter that flies through the universe coursing through our veins. In other words, we are made from the same stuff as creation. Eden sprang from just a few words spoken by our Creator and was called "very good" (Genesis 1:31). It follows then that all creation, including our bodies, is a sacred work of God.

If we want to experience healing and love, a good place to start is *connecting with creation*. It reminds us who we are. Stand in a field, breathe deeply, look toward the heavens, walk through the woods, or consider the thistles around you. You can feel love in creation because it was made by Love.

Jesus taught His disciples to begin their mission by considering the birds of the air and the field of lilies because He understood that the journey to love the world begins with contemplating the Creator of that world. Jesus told them:

Do not worry about your life, what you will eat or drink; or about your body, what you will wear. Is not life more than food, and the body more than clothes? Look at the birds of the air; they do not sow or reap or store away in barns, and yet your heavenly Father feeds them. Are you not much more valuable then they? . . . And why do you worry about clothes? See how the flowers of the field grow. They do not labor or spin. Yet I tell you that not even Solomon in all his splendor was dressed like one of these. (Matthew 6:25–26, 28–29)

The gifts of creation come to us in a million ways; it can take a lifetime of walking and considering to understand all that creation has to offer. The gifts can come in an intentional moment when we stop to smell honeysuckle or by surprise when we hear a song from a bird while sitting quietly on a beach. The gifts can come when we lift our heads to the hills or dip our bodies in a river as a sign of new life. From every animal that finds us, every flower that allows us to glimpse its blossom, every cloud that inspires us—creation's gifts are infinite if we open our eyes to see them.

Make a point to find these healing gifts in your daily routines. When you wake up, instead of reaching for coffee or the Internet, first simply *be*. Listen and look. What do you hear and see? These things are reminders of the presence of the living Spirit of God right beside you.

When you feel frustrated at lines, traffic, and the busyness of the world around you, look and listen again. Can you recognize something healing right in your midst that brings you peace amid stress or a bit of joy in sorrow?

As you drift off to sleep, instead of watching TV or reading as the last act of the day, take five minutes and listen as you close your eyes. Recall the amazing creation you have witnessed, and give thanks for every living thing you encountered.

Another way to connect to creation is to learn about the healing properties of the plants around you. Before modern medicine, tradition told us to use what grew from the earth. To breathe in lavender for peace. To pick some rosemary and set it by your nightstand for help with memory. To put some wild mint in a drink to help settle your stomach.

> **Come, my beloved, let us go to the countryside. . . . Let us go early to the vineyards to see if the vines have budded.**
>
> *Song of Solomon 7:11–12*

Whatever is growing near you, learn about these plants and see how they can be part of healing in your life—not as miracle cures but as part of your intentional walk toward wholeness.

As we consider the gifts of creation, it is good to remember that no plants were considered weeds in Eden. Even some plants we may deem invasive, such as the thistle, carry healing in their essence.

He covers the sky with clouds; he supplies the earth with rain and makes grass grow on the hills.

Psalm 147:8

A Poem for Inspiration

Standing under a hundred-year-old elm
Whose majesty raises my head
With regal canopied scepters,
I whisper, "Here I am."

The muse is lurking in solitude
on lofty branches in prismed light.
Searching for an inspired thought,
I beg, "Come to me."

The muse was waiting in my neighbor's yard
While I roamed the world searching,
Calling out in daily faithfulness,
"I am ready to listen."

I set up camp in his shadowed peace,
But he already flew away.
I am left longing, with a single prayer:
"Come find me again."

There is nowhere in the world you can travel where you can't find thistles, and no one will stop you from picking them. I remember a cold January morning almost ten years ago when I was collecting thistles to turn into paper made from their purple down. I was standing in a huge half-dead field, and as I bent over to cut maybe the hundredth blossom, a man drove by and looked at me with some concern. Seeing myself through his eyes, I laughed and waved at him, realizing how silly I must look hunched over, cutting half-dead weeds. *Oh my goodness,* I thought, *I have become a thistle farmer.*

All of creation can be part of our healing, and nothing needs to be left behind or condemned.

And a moment later, I found myself weeping. I wept as I thought about all the side roads, thorns, and brokenness I had known in my life—the loss of my father and mother, the man who abused me for years, and the times in my youth when I was really lost. I thought about all the mercy and forgiveness people offered that helped me find my way home and into a healing community. And I felt completely and utterly grateful that it all had led me to this place—here, by the side of the road—where I could experience a field of half-dead thistle as a rich and beautiful Eden.

When you can see such a field as rich and beautiful, all of creation looks stunning. All of it can be part of our healing, and nothing needs to be left behind or condemned.

Thistles have become for me a beautiful symbol of healing and grace. In the small space below the blossom and above the dagger thorns is a smooth part where you can hold on to the flower to harvest it. Since the plant is known for its dangerous sharp edges, this smooth spot comes as a sweet surprise, like all grace. Thistles remind us that despite the thorns, creation remains healing and beautiful. They teach us that people, like plants, are all part of that creation, and there is no one we need condemn or leave behind.

Learning to love *all* of creation is an adventure and a surprising walk in grace. Sometimes, if something is common or happens daily, we forget how inspiring it is or that we are looking at God's own handiwork right in front of us. We shouldn't dismiss a sunrise just because it happens every day. We shouldn't let our eyes miss the celebration that is going on around

Healing Properties of Thistles

- Thistle extract is often used to detoxify and restore the liver.
- Drinking thistle tea can be calming after trauma and good for digestion.
- Without thistles, monarch butterflies would starve!
- Thistle down makes strong and beautiful paper.

us. God is found in the wilderness and in the trees that clap their hands as they dance in the wind. We can feel the Spirit when we stroll among the daffodils and wayside wildflowers strewn by distant winds. When we look with new eyes at this incredible gift of creation, we can find the sacred in the ordinary, the miracle in the mundane, and the promise of healing in each day—each extraordinary and holy day.

CHAPTER 2

LOVE HEALS WITH DAILY RITUALS

Practicing healing throughout our day

Turning and Turning

God, set me on the path of healing again.

Turn me to the rising sun when I need to be inspired.

Turn me to wilderness when I need to be lost.

Turn me toward the world when I need to work.

Turn me toward the mountain when I need to retreat

So that in turning I find Your loving grace all around.

It takes all night to raise the sun. The spinning of the earth makes it possible to catch that first glimpse of a sunrise. Every morning brings hope of a new beginning, but we let too many of them slip by.

My head and heart are clearest in the morning. I like to get up while it's still dark and wait with the patient trees and hungry birds for the sun to rise. The night moves from black to gray, then to a soft lavender with hints of pink. Just as golden shafts backlight the clouds and an orange glow begins to grace the horizon, I can feel my spirit rise with the sun. I feel the gift of another day and the hope of a new beginning.

This morning I went outside and felt the sunrise that was offered like a gift wrapped in bands of purple. I saw two beautiful rabbits feasting on clover in my overgrown yard, and a cool breeze kissed my cheek in the midst of the summer heat. I was full of praise and gratitude, and I felt inspired to birth new ideas. This morning I prayed with joy, *Alleluia! Praise God, from whom all blessings flow.*

But not yesterday. Yesterday there was another mass shooting in America, someone in our Thistle Farms community relapsed (after she had survived rape and being shot by her pimp), and a storm hid the sunrise. Yesterday I felt anxiety about death after visiting three people who were sick in the hospital. Yesterday was hard. On those days, I need to learn that then, too, I must practice all my daily rituals in faith. Then, too, I need to sing "Alleluia" even as I weep.

Sunrises help me learn to do this. They remind me that healing can be beautifully simple and surprisingly accessible. Healing can happen in both dramatic and small ways. The healing we are seeking for our lives and for the world is something we can experience through a commitment to daily practices that lead us toward wholeness.

These ancient rituals are found in Scripture and in the testimony of faithful men and women. When practiced regularly, they help us discover how love heals us.

- **Reading Scripture.** Finding new life in living words gives us hope.
- **Praying the psalms.** Every sort of condition of humanity is addressed in the words of the psalmists, and we can use them to pray.
- **Breaking bread together.** Either through the Lord's Supper or offering grace at every meal, we remember that everything we eat is a gift from God.
- **Fasting.** This tradition of going without food focuses us and helps us set intentions. It helps our discipline when practiced with prayer.
- **Washing feet.** This was an act in which Jesus told us we would

be disciples. As part of a faith community, it is an intimate and humbling way to offer love to another.

- **Anointing**. As with so many instances in the Bible, anointing is the application of healing oils as a sign of repentance, gratitude, or petition.
- **Laying on hands**. This tradition echoes the church after Pentecost, when Peter and John laid their hands on newly baptized Christians: "And they received the Holy Spirit" (Acts 8:17). When we lay on hands as a community, we invite the Spirit in.
- **Walking**. Taking time to exercise and experience a trail or path frees your mind and settles your spirit. Sometimes it's easier to pray when our feet are moving.
- **Lighting incense**. This tradition is as old as Moses. As the frankincense rises, we can envision our prayers lifting as the aroma cleanses our thoughts and we are invited into silent prayer.

Some of these practices are best done daily, such as reading, walking, and praying; others are best done at regular points during the year, such as fasting and washing feet. Look to church traditions, calendars, or your own schedule, and think of ways to weave some of these ancient practices into your life.

Look to the LORD
and his strength;
seek his face always.

1 Chronicles 16:11

The good news of healing is that the oldest wisdom in the world really works. We don't have to reinvent the processes of love or healing, and it is not out of our reach. We simply do basic things every day with unwavering discipline—things that help us slowly but surely grow into who we were made to be.

Our understanding of how love heals evolves and deepens as we practice daily. And learning what works best for each of us also takes time and practice. It's like preparing to run a marathon: we start training for a few miles a day and then come to an understanding of how we can best train our bodies for the long race. That awareness helps us, as the apostle Paul famously put it, "Run in such a way as to get the prize. Everyone who competes in the games goes into strict training. They do it to get a crown that

---

Here are more simple ways to incorporate healing into our modern lives:

- Eating healthier
- Having some fun
- Getting off social media
- Giving generously
- Volunteering

- Singing
- Lighting candles
- Sipping tea
- Practicing yoga
- Learning something new

will not last, but we do it to get a crown that will last forever. Therefore I do not run like someone running aimlessly" (1 Corinthians 9:24–26). In a world of aimlessness, we train ourselves through ritual.

My mornings are grounded in ritual. In the dawn's early moments, I light a candle, and it invites me to breathe. I begin my morning prayers and anoint my hands and face with a bit of lavender and moringa oil. Then I sip a cup of tea made by women in our social enterprises, and I either walk, do yoga stretches, or take a bath and begin to write. It took me years to figure out this routine. I read about what other people did, I tried on different ways of preparing for my day, and slowly, over time, my daily healing rituals took shape.

Afterward, I am ready to get my kids to school, meet the women of Thistle Farms, take the time to listen to colleagues, and focus on loving the world one person at a time. Sometimes I still get lazy, sidetracked, and frustrated, and I want to call a mulligan on the day. But mostly I stick to the practice, and the practice makes room for everything else in my day.

Being busy is no excuse. Everybody is busy. The key is deciding what you are going to be busy doing and making space for that. It might mean dinners are simpler, clothes don't get folded as often, and you miss out on other activities, but for folks like me who can spin out and lose focus, morning rituals are grounding and essential.

We can all find ways to incorporate healing practices throughout the day, through even the smallest actions: how we greet another person, how we say a prayer before we get in the car, or how we say good night. It's a matter of becoming aware that with every action, we can practice being more peaceful and prayerful and more loving and compassionate toward ourselves and others. We don't always act because we feel like it. We act because of who we want to become. And we pray for what we hope to become. That is what makes faith a journey. In the small steps we make daily, we find, looking back, that we have made a big difference.

Old-Time Religion

Daily practices remind me of a song from the late nineteenth century, "Give Me That Old Time Religion." It's a mantra to hum while we explore how to respond to universal injustices and personal pain. That old-time religion "was tried in the fiery furnace" . . . it "makes me love everybody . . . it's good enough for me." We remember that others have gone through what we are experiencing. Others didn't know the road before them. Others felt loneliness and pain. The old wounds humanity carries demand that we respond with love, the oldest and deepest truth of religion.

Thistle Farms is full of daily rituals that change lives. We start every day sitting in a circle and lighting a candle. The candle is made by women survivors, and when we light it we say, "We light this candle for the woman still on the streets, we light this candle for the woman trying to find her

way home, and we light this candle because a single candle can cut a path through the darkest night." Then we begin our day of making essential oils that bring healing and products that allow us to talk about women's freedom, to change our culture, and to enable communities of women to be economically independent.

We need some good old-time religious practices to infuse our lives so we can use the most powerful force—*love*—to heal our communities. Practices teach us to habitually invite God to strengthen and shape us so we can become disciples capable of embracing the backside of anger, the shadow side of pain, the short side of justice, and the inside of prison walls with love. If we practice daily, we will get stronger and stronger in our faith and commitment. We can trust God to transform our brokenness into compassion and empower us to offer love without judgment. That love can be cast wide enough to reach those suffering in the streets and entrenched in prisons.

> **It is good to praise the LORD and make music to your name, O Most High, proclaiming your love in the morning and your faithfulness at night.**
>
> *Psalm 92:1–2*

One of our survivor-leaders grasped this reality one day as we were standing at our Thistle Farms booth at a national convention. Through serious daily practices, she had been working for more than two years on her healing from abuse, prostitution, and addiction. She had worked a twelve-step program, met weekly with counselors, sat in the circle and lit candles at Thistle Farms, and found her own ways of learning to heal daily. She had gone back to school, worked to save money to buy a car, and reconciled with her family. Now she was part of the travel team, selling our healing oils and candles and explaining how our community functions. She was amazed as person after person walked up to the booth, bought items, gave us blessings, and shared their own stories. After a few days, when several hundred people had talked to us, she turned to me and said, "I finally get it. This healing takes a while. And after it takes place, I realize it's not about me; it's about us. I am here so another woman can find her way home."

It takes a while for the truth of healing and love to sink into our hearts, and it takes a daily practice to understand healing love's depth and power. It takes that old-time religion that practices love every day.

Practice is nine-tenths of love. Love is experienced, felt, and spoken loudest in our daily practices with ourselves, one another, and the world. The old phrase is, "Don't tell me you love me. Show me." One of the most powerful examples of this in Scripture is after the resurrection, when Jesus asked Peter, "Do you love Me" (John 21:17)? After Peter told him he did, Jesus asked him to show that love by feeding His sheep. In other words, if you love God, care for the children of God.

To feed His sheep, and to feed yourself, find out what works for you. Dig deeper into your heart to discover how to pray more fervently, how to serve more boldly, and how to love more lavishly. God's healing grace comes more readily as we do the daily work of being disciples—on good days and bad days, when the sun is bright and when the sky is stormy. That is how we embody the love we long to feel.

We keep at it step-by-step, through long nights when our fears tell us the morning will not come again and when we feel disheartened by the injustices of the world or weariness within. We keep going. We light another candle. We read a psalm. We wait for the sunrise. It is coming.

CHAPTER 3

LOVE HEALS BESIDE STILL WATERS

Learning to find peace

Still Mountain Lake

Her silky water reflects landscape in watercolor perfection.

Clouds sail past like four-masted ships on her canvas.

Wind becomes incarnate, rippling her surface.

The thimbleweed and delphinium share the shoreline

Where we come to her curved borders to quench longing.

The faithful pine and aspen suitors watch over her.

We are parched for her life-giving water formed

in the mystery of mountains and carried down canyon aisles.

Mica adorns her with hints of jade that add to her calm majesty.

Silt and mud sink at her feet in quiet repose;

their glacial journey long ago laid to rest.

She laughs as rainbow trout swim in her belly,

hungry for the next hatch of flies she offers with grace.

Breathing in thin air makes you dizzy with dreams.

In her deep black eyes, you look perfectly young again and know—

this is why you come to her still waters.

When the events of our lives get us stirred up, the waters get muddy. All the silt and dirt of anxiety swirls around, and we can't see clearly. Take a glass. Pour in some beautiful, pure water. Then stir in a bit of dirt and try to look through the glass. It's not until we set the glass down and let the dirt settle that we can see through the water. In the same way, we work through troubled waters, and we wait, and then we finally see clearly the path before us. We patiently use our cultivated daily practices when times are rough, and then suddenly, one day, the skies open up and we find peace and healing like an unexpected gift. Love heals as we calm ourselves and make room to feel revived.

When we sit beside still waters, we can remember all that healing is possible in our lives. In the Twenty-third Psalm, we are reminded that though we walk in the shadows of death, God leads us to quiet waters. We can't run away from the trouble, so we are called to sit still with that trouble and be calmed by our Lord, who never abandons us—even when we are neck-deep in turbulent, wild waters.

In the Gospels, Jesus took the disciples to "a quiet place" as the crowds pushed in and the work intensified (Mark 6:31). They went to find healing in the quiet. Like the disciples, we need to find places to quiet ourselves and be led to peace.

Go find a green pasture, sit on a pew, stretch out on an exercise mat, soak in a bathtub—go anywhere that is your quiet space so you can get still enough to hear the voice of God again. Even the prophet Elijah had to wait

Love heals as we
calm ourselves
and make room
to feel revived.

for the storm to pass in front of him to hear God's still, small voice: "After the earthquake came a fire, but the LORD was not in the fire. And after the fire came a gentle whisper" (1 Kings 19:12).

I have been pastoring a chapel for twenty-five years and running a global community at the same time, so finding still waters is critical. The old saying is that "Preachers preach what they most need to hear." So I preach to the congregants and teach women I work with that learning to find still waters helps them on their own healing journeys. That is the lesson I need to hear most. After the craziness of the earthquakes of pastoring and the fire of running a large social enterprise, it is in the whisper of prayer that I find my way to love again. Living in peace is critical to recovering from trauma, and it keeps us close to the heart of faith.

A Habit of Peace

I have been practicing waking up to prayer, doing an hour of yoga or Pilates, and walking a few miles five days a week. I go whether I am inspired to or not. I go because I know that when I walk or exercise, I breathe and settle the noise around me. I go because I know when I walk in the woods or pray silently early in the morning, all the clatter of everyone else's agendas grows quiet. Of course, some days I go out and come home, and I barely remember what I did. I go through the motions, make my path in a circle through the woods, and the worries and fears are still stirred up within me. But every now and then, everything settles and the still waters surround me. And I am so thankful I didn't miss it.

In the midst of a world filled with stress, it's critical to search for peace to quiet our souls. We can respond to stress by finding our quiet times where we feel found, not lost. Moments of peace can be fleeting and far between, but they are a healing balm for a troubled heart. Times when we see birds overhead, or we hear a hymn sung with perfect harmony, or we see the love of God reflected in a child's eyes are so temporal. But they sit us down by an eternal moment so all that troubles us can pass and we can feel peace. In such moments, all we can do is give thanks that the Holy Spirit leads us still to calming and peaceful waters.

One morning before I was going to preach in North Carolina, I got a text message from one of the Thistle Farms graduates: "Today I woke up and heard the birds and felt peace. Thank you." That simple note meant the world to me. She was finding those still waters where we can reflect— where we get quiet enough to hear the birds.

Lost Sheep and Muddy Waters

Even with our practices, even with reflection, the truth is that most of the time, our waters are pretty muddy and we feel lost. Jesus knows us well, and He spoke about how a loving shepherd always goes and searches for the ones who are lost: "What do you think? If a man owns a hundred sheep, and one of them wanders away, will he not leave the ninety-nine on the hills and go to look for the one that wandered off?" (Matthew 18:12).

We wander in wild places as lonely as the fields near Galilee, where scrub brush is scattered with wild geranium and thistles on sandy soil. Those are the times when, even though the psalmist says we shall fear no evil, we still get pretty scared. When we are lost, we search, and it's hard to see ahead when everything is clouded with dust. We can't seem to find our way through or understand what the next right step is to make better decisions. In those muddy waters and dry fields, Jesus calls to us and to all who are hurting or lost. He says simply to pray and keep going—you will be found.

> **"Ask and it will be given to you; seek and you will find; knock and the door will be opened to you."**
>
> *Matthew 7:7*

Look back at the times when you have felt lost and realized later that the Lord was with you the whole way. The practice of reflection can help you peer through those waters and feel more peaceful about any present stress. When we remember that we have been the lost sheep who have been found over and over, we become part of the good news. In parables like the story of the good Samaritan, we know the gratitude of the guy in the ditch (Luke 10:25–37). We know the freedom of forgiveness experienced by a woman caught in adultery as Jesus wiped all judgment away or the wonder of love's healing power with mud on blind eyes (John 8:1–11; 9:1–11).

I was lost by the time I started first grade. It was a leader in the church who stepped in to "help" my family after my father was killed when I was five. His intrusion into our family began my two years wandering in the lonely fields of sexual abuse.

I learned in those moments of grief and trauma that most sheep don't wander off; they are often pushed out of the fold by the silence kept in dysfunctional communities. They're swept away by devastating poverty and by overwhelming universal injustices that render communities numb. The feeling of being lost was devastating, and peace was a rare commodity for years.

But loving communities, prayer, mercy, and forgiveness helped me beyond anything I could have done myself. They helped me to find some peaceful waters along the way. I was lost—really lost—but because of those loving communities, I have been led back to still waters throughout my life.

Pulled Back In

I met Katrina in Rwanda, where Thistle Farms sources our geranium oil. She had lived in the muddy waters of trauma and grief for more than a decade. She had lost children in the genocide of 1994, endured violence, and lost all she had. She was left wandering like a lost sheep. She had no home and no money and had to beg for food in her village. The community of Ikirezi—started by Dr. Nicholas Hitimana in early 2000 to help the widows of genocide—found her. And "slowly by slowly" (an old African expression), Katrina began to revive the hope deep within her. Through faith and hard work, some of those turbulent waters began to still.

Katrina started working the fields every day. She received a home and a cow in payment for her work. Then she began to work with others to cope with the horrible suffering she had known. Dr. Nicholas Hitimana recently came for a visit and brought a picture of her. In it Katrina is wearing a beautiful African wrap and speaking to a group of farmers about the upcoming crop. While saltwater tears probably still sting her eyes and cloud her vision, you can see a reborn peace and calmness in her. You can feel the healing emanating from a woman who has done the hard work of waiting for still waters during some of the greatest storms humanity can inflict. Nicholas told me that Katrina now has two relatives living with her and that they have beautiful and plentiful gardens to help others who are in need of food in the village.

Meeting women like Katrina reminds me of why I started this work. I founded the Thistle Farms community in true gratitude for all the mercy I had known. I wanted to serve other women who felt like lost sheep and who had endured more than I could ever imagine as survivors of trafficking and addiction. Over the past twenty years, the women of Thistle Farms have demonstrated that it is not that difficult to join in the work of finding lost sheep and guiding brothers and sisters toward still waters. It can be as simple as offering a bag of chips to someone who is hungry, visiting a prison, or saying, "Welcome home." I have learned the truth that without one another, we are all lost. Together, as grateful, found sheep in Jesus' flock, we become a powerful and healing fold.

Still-Water Habits

One way you can intentionally still the troubled waters and take notice of God's still, small voice is through simple prayer—a simple prayer that can make a huge difference and be done as you are taking care of the wants and needs of others along the way. Try it and see if it helps you see more clearly through your glass. Pray in silence with the fifteen-hundred-year-old Christian tradition called *contemplative prayer*. In this practice you commit to twenty minutes of prayer with a single word or phrase that keeps you calm and focused. You can use a Bible verse, a single word, or even a phrase like, "God, You are so good to me."

Other ways to cultivate the still-water habits throughout the day might include:

- Reading and meditating on God's holy Word
- Carving out time alone (in the bathtub, in the car, in the woods)

- Reflecting on how grateful you are for small things
- Taking a bit of time away for renewal
- Spending time in a worship setting that calms your spirit
- Journaling even just a few sentences a day for reflection
- Sharing an inspired thought with someone to help them when they feel lost

Through habits, faith, and prayer, it is possible for all of us to find waters still enough to help us remember with gratitude all the healing we have known, no matter how lost we have been. We can go to the places and people that call us into a deep calm, that allow us to feel found. In those spaces we can sing the words of "Amazing Grace," we can breathe in the Spirit of peace, and we can feel revived. That is the gift of still waters on the healing journey.

A Psalm to Calm the Waters

My heart is not proud, LORD,
    my eyes are not haughty;
I do not concern myself with great matters
    or things too wonderful for me.
But I have calmed and quieted myself,
    I am like a weaned child with its mother;
like a weaned child I am content.

PSALM 131:1–2

CHAPTER 4

LOVE HEALS WITH COMPASSION

Nourishing connections between us

A Prayer for Compassion

Give me eyes to see that You are the person in front of me who is
hungry, gracious Lord. When I fail to see my neighbor as myself,
cure my blindness. When I fail to hear Your voice when a friend
is speaking from their brokenness, give me ears to hear.
When I can't feel empathy for the stranger who is afraid, kindle my
heart to comfort. In all things, mold me to be more compassionate
as a follower of Your ways. Remind me again that in loving one
another, we all find our way to You. Amen.

The space between having everything and having nothing isn't vast. The journey between the wilderness and Jerusalem may be shorter than we think. The line that separates the givers and receivers is thin. The connections between all of us are greater than anything that separates us, and when we see them, our brokenness begins to be transformed into compassion for others and even for ourselves.

Compassion is one of the most important attributes of love. When we cultivate compassion for others, we can feel the loving-kindness God offers to us. In other words, instead of dismissing others' brokenness, we engage suffering with hope. A daily commitment to compassion gives us the ability to feel the joys and sorrows of others and be gentle with ourselves.

Cultivating compassion for ourselves and others doesn't require making drastic changes or giving up our lives as we know them. It means that we remember healing is possible for all people. It means asking the question, "What happened to you?" instead of, "What is wrong with you?" It means inviting someone's story and listening to it with gentle ears. Cultivating compassion means we don't dismiss entire groups of people for any reason, and we don't let cynicism guide our actions and speech. It also means we don't give up on others—even if it feels like it's going to be a long, hard journey toward healing.

I learned about how powerfully compassion translates into healing from one of the great survivor-leaders at Thistle Farms, whose story unfolded over fifteen years. Katrina came into the community after a childhood that was filled with love but also included an abusive stepfather. That abuse led her to the streets and into addiction and trafficking. When she came into the community, she had a beautiful daughter, Ebony, who would sometimes join her mom at the community meetings.

At one of those meetings, while we were working on the skill of building financial stability, the facilitator passed out index cards and asked the participants to draw their dreams on the cards. She told the participants that if they could draw their goals, they could work toward making them come true. Ebony whispered to her mom, "Draw a house, Momma. Draw a house."

The next year, Katrina became the first national sales director for the Thistle Farms social enterprise, which she would help build into the largest of its kind in the United States. Two years later, she built her daughter a house. She said receiving so much compassion *from* others gave her a deep longing to be compassionate *to* others. She has always invited people who needed a helping hand into her house and has continued to go back to the streets to help other women. She serves as a mentor to women new to recovery. After Katrina married, she and her husband adopted a six-year-old boy. The compassion Katrina once received at her lowest point came back into the world in marvelous ways. And she raised her daughter, Ebony, to practice the same tireless compassion.

When Ebony graduated from college, Katrina hired her to be our sales rep for the largest chain store that carries our products. Ebony always

When we cultivate compassion for others, we can feel the loving-kindness God offers to us.

treats the women on her sales team with loving-kindness. In 2016, that large chain store invited Ebony to come to California to speak to their entire sales team. Ebony talked about what a compassionate community had meant for her family. She said that even when she and her mom had nothing, people cared. And now she and her mom were working as part of a global effort to help one woman at a time, with compassion for all.

When Ebony stood to speak, she spoke as a receiver of compassion. She reminded the sales team that they, too, could play a part in welcoming more and more women into healing community. Ebony's sales pitch was a story of brokenness and compassion coming full circle, and it sparked a deep reaction in her audience. The sales team tripled the number of stores that carried our products. They saw how they could help; they connected with compassion. And now the cycle continues.

> **When he went ashore he saw a great crowd, and he had compassion on them and healed their sick.**
>
> *Matthew 14:14* ESV

Compassionate love breaks through barriers between people. No matter how any of us got to where we are, we are always in a good spot to learn about love, and our hearts will respond to it powerfully. Compassion means we learn to recognize ourselves in others, as the sales team did with Ebony. When we learn about the horrific journeys that refugees, survivors, and prisoners have made, we remember we are capable of helping—and we are in a position to help in a particular way. Even if all we have is dirt and spit, we can learn to make a healing mud to soothe wounds, like Jesus did to restore sight to the blind (John 9:6). Compassion moves us to step into the fearful places where we worry and despair. It gives us strength to take up our cross to bear another's burdens.

A Prayer of Thanksgiving for the Walk We Have Been Given

Show us how to love our walk and to give thanks for each step. Give us compassion for all those who walk beside us, and help us remember everyone who taught us how to walk. Let wisdom be the gift on this walk so that we can show others how to follow this path. You always raise up laborers for Your harvest of love; let us be sowers with faithful steps and boundless seeds so that love can flourish around us. Amen.

Compassion for Others

Jesus said, "Take up [your] cross . . . and follow me" (Luke 9:23). That is the call to feel deep compassion for the sake of others. At first glance, that may look like a huge wooden burden we are supposed to drag around on our backs. But when I think about bearing our crosses as disciples, I think those crosses start out small. They are as small as a seed of compassion for others. When we pick up that seed and plant it, compassion grows into something beautiful and powerful that we couldn't have imagined when we started. Many saints and leaders of movements over centuries describe faith as a long journey we take one step at a time. St. Ignatius, the founder of the Jesuits, praised God for each step. "Grant that your love may so fill our lives," he prayed, "that we may count nothing too small to do for you, nothing too much to give, and nothing too hard to bear. . . . Teach me to serve you as you deserve; to give, and not to count the cost." Our journeys with crosses start small and then grow into something beautiful.

On my first annual trip to Ecuador in 1998, I was walking in the fields when I stumbled upon a tiny kindergarten building that had closed because of lack of support. I felt compassion for that small group of kids and had a simple thought: *We could reopen this one-room school. How hard could it be?* Over the years, as the community I serve in Nashville nurtured relationships and expanded on that thought, ideas grew, and the project took on weight. One person suggested a medical clinic; then someone else suggested a library; and another mentioned establishing a new women's social enterprise. One proposed, "Maybe we should dig a well." On and on, people had ideas. Then it seemed that all of a sudden a great vision was realized—a new commitment and a new life—and it continues to grow in beautifully exponential ways.

Nineteen years later, these small seeds of compassion have grown into a school that now serves seven grades, a medical clinic that sees a thousand people annually, a social enterprise of women survivors who design and sew clerical robes and linens, and an ongoing community of hundreds of new friends from across the globe. Compassion allows us to give and receive love so that we become more loving disciples.

Weighing the Cross You Bear

How can you tell whether you are carrying a cross or a ball and chain? If you are struggling with the idea of carrying a certain cross of compassion for others, reflect on these simple questions. Then prayerfully search for the next step forward in cross-bearing.

- Did the cross you're bearing begin with a seed of compassion?
- Can you bear it with joy?
- Does it bring gratitude to your faith?
- Does the cost of bearing it diminish in comparison to the love it produces?
- Do you share the cross with others?
- Does the privilege of bearing your cross outweigh the fear of getting involved?

That's how it is in your daily commitment—your compassion leads you not to pick up some horrible burden but simply to fall in love. That's what taking up your cross means: it means you are falling in love. It means you are becoming the disciple you were meant to be. It's not about gloom and doom for us.

Our daily commitments and callings should bring joy and gratitude. If your daily callings and commitments don't bring you joy, they're not a cross you're bearing. They're a ball and chain. Cut it loose. Our cross should stem from compassion for others and produce deep gratitude for the things that mean the most in our lives. It should remind us what we are willing to bear for the sake of love. That compassion ties us to each other in love, and it tells us we are not alone.

Compassion for Ourselves

When I founded Thistle Farms twenty years ago, I met a woman named Regina, who was living on the streets after experiencing much trauma in her youth. She was a survivor of addiction, prostitution, and trafficking, and she was the mother of three young boys. Yet in small, profound ways, she was the first woman in this community who began to teach me that you can't kill hope in people. You can abuse, jail, sell, and assault people, but you can't kill their hope.

In 1997, shortly after we opened the first house, I stopped by and saw through the window that Regina was dancing. When I went inside and asked her why she was dancing, she said she was having a Holy Ghost party. We laughed then, but after I went back to my car, I sat for a while, crying. I cried because I wanted to believe that in spite of all the pain and brokenness in this world, love is more powerful and forgiveness runs deeper. I cried because I knew my cross—my work with Thistle Farms—was going to take up so much of my life. And I cried because I couldn't remember the last time I had danced with the Holy Spirit. Those tears were a sign of compassion for myself. They were healing tears that sprang from seeing Regina's joy and knowing that this work was a way for me to learn to dance with the Spirit again.

> **Put on then, as God's chosen ones, holy and beloved, compassionate hearts, kindness, humility, meekness, and patience, bearing with one another and, if one has a complaint against another, forgiving each other; as the Lord has forgiven you, so you also must forgive.**
>
> *Colossians 3:12–13 ESV*

Regina went on to help another two hundred women come off the streets. She is now one of the national education directors for the more than sixty communities working to help survivors around the country. For a couple years, she even helped me raise my three young sons.

Regina shows me how it is possible for us to take up our crosses and follow love. Her cross came from trauma that became a life-threatening addiction, and I am so grateful to her that she had enough compassion for herself to bear it. Her full-circle journey helped teach me that there is less pain in bearing our crosses for the sake of love than in not knowing love at all. Regina preaches that when we have compassion for our own stories and brokenness, it is possible to dance with the Holy Spirit and offer compassion to others.

The Cross-Bearing Community

It seems counterintuitive to think that our cross is our healing, but that is what the Gospels teach us. Jesus said, "Whoever wants to save their life will lose it, but whoever loses their life for me will save it" (Luke 9:24). The Gospels also teach us that while we do so much of our work alone, there is also a communal element to the saving, compassionate work of bearing crosses! Cross bearing is not just an individual task. Your daily commitment—the calling that moves you—is not just on you; it's the task of a community. Christ was speaking to a community, and He still is: "For where two or three gather in my name, there am I with them" (Matthew 18:20).

If you think an injustice is your burden to carry or your calling is only on you, you've missed the point. Part of bearing a cross is learning how to share the journey with others and remembering that we carry our crosses together. We all share a calling to love the world. It fills us with gratitude and joy and gives us a way to live.

Teachers like Katrina, Ignatius, and Regina remind us that compassion for ourselves and others offers healing and joy. Every person you meet has a story, and it is *always* worth listening to. In others' stories, we remember that the lines between priests and prostitutes are infinitesimally small. The lines that separate us are wiped out in the sand of the compassion we give to one another.

CHAPTER 5

LOVE HEALS ACROSS THE WORLD

Branching into new territory

Coming Full Circle

The sun rises in the east

As delicately as gray turns to lavender.

She sweeps across the great wall in a single bound

Then arches over pyramids, temples, and deserts.

She stretches her arms over the ocean,

Peeks over mountains, and graces the valleys

As she dances with clouds over prairie.

She begins her dive toward evening on Pacific islands,

Dipping beneath an old volcanic hill.

Her benediction blushes with unbridled joy

As she slips past the west in faithfulness.

The distance between *here* and *there* sometimes feels impossible to traverse. Healing, though, is a universal pilgrimage that we all long to make, and so we have to try to cover the distance. When I pray for the health and safety of those I love, I recognize that it is a universal prayer spoken across the world. Because of this universal nature of prayer, healing is an integrated chain; it is realized as everyone in that chain feels cared for. If I am working at Thistle Farms to create a healing tea or oil, it needs to be healing not just for the person drinking the tea or being anointed—it also needs to be healing for the people producing, manufacturing, and distributing the tea and oil. We have the responsibility and joy of taking care of one another.

Globalization affects our economy, our local businesses, our jobs, our environment. Economics, religion, and politics travel freely across borders with the click of a button, and transportation is more accessible than ever before. But certain things have always been "global"—we have always been connected. Across seas, time, and cultures, we are all part of the same world.

Jesus said, "I am the vine; you are the branches. If you remain in me and I in you, you will bear much fruit" (John 15:5). We are called to remain together through our mutual connection to the vine, to branch out and bear the fruit of healing. Whether we physically extend our branches to faraway places or connect closer to home with those from different lands, we can reach over barriers. We can help bring God's healing love to the most broken corners of our world—and of our own communities.

For God, nothing is "foreign." Love heals across the world, and God is everywhere. We are not being simplistic when we sing the children's song "He's Got the Whole World in His Hands." We are remembering that God does indeed hold the whole world and longs for every one of us to find our healing, together. It is a universal truth that love is woven into the fabric of creation and is a part of how all communities heal. I once heard a friend say that Jesus offers absolute healing and forgiveness for the whole world. That may be the simplest way of proclaiming that beautiful truth: "He's got you and me, sister, in His hands."

Tighter Connection, More Healing

When I think of Thistle Farms's global partner in Ghana, I remember sitting at a small table with them, sharing a meal. When I didn't finish my food, a young woman who worked for the partner organization took my plate to the kitchen, and I could see her eat everything off it before washing it. It humbled me for sure, but it also bonded me to her in our common work. If I can know that what we do together helps her—specifically, to find food in this big wide world—I know I am part of her healing. We at Thistle Farms want to stay connected to the producers and support their

work because we want to be part of the chain of healing—from the young women recovering from trauma and poverty to those who sell the products across the world to those who use the oils or give them as gifts.

It is daunting to try to love the whole world one person at a time, but that is the task of being a disciple. In the world of human trafficking, I can think about the young woman in Ghana hungry for the scraps off my plate and know that what I do here in the United States matters to her. We all can love the world through our interactions, our business choices, our lifestyle choices, and how we choose to spend our time. It's easy to dismiss this by telling ourselves that the small things, like buying fair trade or smiling at a neighbor, can't make any difference in the great suffering of the world. It's hard to imagine that our small acts change the balance of love in the world. Yet it is even harder to imagine the world being a more loving place if we do nothing. In our small sacrificial choices, we show that we love the world. It takes a great deal of humility to face universal issues by simply loving the next person who crosses our path.

It takes a great deal of humility to face universal issues by simply loving the next person who crosses our path.

It is harsh out there in the world, and all of us have heard war stories. Yet everywhere I've traveled over the last twenty years, I have seen this truth: people across the globe in loving and compassionate communities *do* recover and find freedom. Believing—and seeing—that healing happens across oceans and over chasms makes us all more hopeful about the world we live in. In the twenty-one countries where we work with women, we have experienced that the tighter our connections across the world are, the more exponentially love's healing power grows. Not only do the markets increase so that each woman is more economically independent and can buy school clothes and groceries, but whole communities around these social entrepreneurs change as well.

Thistle Farms began working with a small social enterprise that started in the mountains of Mexico in 2014. I am filled with joy when I hear their stories of how the community is embracing the once-homeless and outcast women. The five women have found markets to sell their products and are welcomed into stores. They've put their children in schools, and the education system is helping them integrate with grace. Local handymen and churches have jumped in to offer help when needed. Each woman dreams of the same things any woman survivor in the world does—that her children will be spared what she endured, that she will have access to good health care, that she can maintain a safe home and find a loving partner. When we buy into the truth that love heals across the globe, we are given the ability to see healing flourish in spaces where women were once cast out on the streets.

How to Branch Out

Even if we don't travel overseas, our lives are integrated into the whole world, from the clothes we put on our backs to the tea or coffee we consume to the Google searches we initiate. Wherever we are, we all have access to places that need healing. In your town, in your state, in your country, are people from faraway lands, people who long to be connected to loving community. True, it isn't easy to reach out past our comfortable boundaries to create change across the world, or even in our own backyard. It can be messy and sometimes awkward to try to start a conversation with language or cultural barriers. We often don't know what to do or how to begin. Yet I have found the following three things useful when crossing into new territory, whether you are traveling across the seas or meeting someone on the street.

1. Humility

Since none of us fully knows the culture of lands foreign to us, it's important to take a stance of listening and learning as you meet someone from another place. Whether it's a neighbor, a classmate, a cab driver, or a new member of a church community, ask simple questions and be willing to read about the history of their country. The Scriptures remind us that our spiritual ancestors were wandering Arameans: "My ancestor Jacob was a wandering Aramean who went to live as a foreigner in Egypt. His family arrived few in number, but in Egypt they became a large and mighty nation" (Deuteronomy 26:5 NLT).

In other words, at some point in our lineage, we have all been lost and were searching for some hospitality as we made a new home. Have some humility and compassion for what your new neighbor must be going through, and offer a welcome that graces us all.

2. Humor

We will trip over our words and make some blunders about race, ethnicity, religion, and language. Don't let the fear of a faux pas keep you from engaging in new relationships that can be healing for everyone. When I first journeyed to Ecuador in 1998, my Spanish was so bad that after I said anything, people would ask me to repeat it while they brought a couple of friends over so they could hear my "Southern" Spanish. We would all laugh, and then I would try again. My Spanish hasn't really improved that much in the last two decades, but the laughter over my inability to speak well has bonded me to several people in that community forever. We are friends on Facebook, we see each other every year, we know each other's families, and we share a mutual commitment to improving the lives of women and children in their community and in mine. The humor we've shared has been a large part of the healing we have offered one another.

3. Respect

It is good to remember that the histories that created solid borders, separate governments, and distinct groups are formidable, and we may not see change in our lifetimes. But the goal of reaching across the globe is not to change the world; it is to be willing to change ourselves so we can love it better. That means taking a posture of respect by listening and hearing new ideas that might help us make a small change in the way we think or feel. It is not a false respect; it is a deeply rooted respect for another's story. When I traveled, I used to think privately that Thistle Farms was bringing needed change to a community through clinics, education, or social enterprise. *If they could just understand how to do it my way!* was the disrespectful and anti-gospel thought underlying some of my efforts. I wanted access to health care for more moms and babies as well as freedom from sexual assault and the violence of poverty for more people. Those are beautiful things to want for another community. But I learned that I first have to listen, learn about, and respect another place and be a part of it to love it well. Once I began to practice love and be open to the change needed for all of us, our work was more meaningful. I have learned so much and have so much more to learn.

We are part of the human family. The Scriptures teach us in John 3:16 that "God so loved the [whole] world." God loves us wherever we are, and no matter where we travel, God meets us there. There is no place that God is not. There is no place too vast and no chasm too wide for God to build a bridge over.

A Prayer for Seeking

Lord, You have made us in Your image. Teach us to see this day, every person we meet, whether on the streets or in the mirror, as Your incarnate face. All our journeys begin and end with You—now we need to learn how to travel close to You on our way home. Help us seek and knock to find You wherever we are. Let us feel the cloud of witnesses that assures us of Your guiding hand. Whether we lie down in green pastures or walk in the valley of the shadow of death, let us feel You leading us and holding us fast. Amen.

The goal of reaching across the globe is not to change the world; it is to change ourselves so we can love it better.

Crossing Borders Where You Are

- Take the time to research the products and food you buy as a family.
- Make a note of what you can change to support loving trade practices.
- Get involved in global missions in your church.
- Pray for all the victims of war.
- Find out which schools in your area are serving immigrant populations, and see if they have a need that you or your church could help meet.
- Read more history and study maps!
- Find out which agencies in your city are welcoming refugees and how to participate in small ways, like writing a note of welcome or gathering supplies.
- Read about how governments are spending foreign assistance, and see how it promotes your understanding of loving the world.

CHAPTER 6

LOVE HEALS ON THE EDGES OF OUR HEARTS

Growing through painful spaces

The Edges of My Heart

Sitting on a smooth stone by the river,

Formed by wind and time for weary pilgrims,

I watch birds, fish, and lupine dance on wind.

I hardly move as endless water rushes.

It looks as if I am doing nothing,

maybe wasting time . . .

that could be spent more industriously

feeding the poor or folding laundry.

Instead I travel toward my heart.

I take in memory for sustenance

and let imagination be my northern star.

Rapids of worry catch my breath.

I abandon shame and fear as sinking weights

as the current pulls against the edges of my heart.

I taste tears of familiar longing

I have carried from my youth.

I feel the freedom of a new idea

born in a heart created for more than beating.

The rock under me has not moved.

The birds and flowers still dance

as my heart swells along the river's edge.

After we have connected to creation, committed to daily practices, found still waters, and cultivated compassion at home and abroad, it seems possible to come home to ourselves. Coming home to ourselves means it is safe to explore deep or scary places like the wounded parts of our hearts. It's easy to ignore these places, to keep busy and distracted, but we'll never find healing for our hearts that way. If we avoid feeling longing or pain, we will continue to try to fill up our lives with things that leave us hungry. We each long for God's love and healing like a deer longs for a babbling brook. But how do we begin to face the broken aspects of our story that live in our memories, our bodies, and still have power to shape us? We don't have to know our way into our hearts; we can trust that the Holy Spirit, the Comforter, is sufficient to guide us toward healing.

Love is our deepest desire, both to give and to receive. That desire is rooted in us and pushes at the edges of our hearts—the places where we grow our capacity to love and to be loved. Jesus talked about this place in Scripture throughout His farewell discourse in the Gospel of John. He told the disciples, "Do not let your hearts be troubled and do not be afraid" (14:27). He saw the ragged edges in the disciples' hearts as they looked into a future without His physical presence. They were scared and heartbroken.

"You are filled with grief because I have said these things," He said (16:6). Yet Jesus told them He would not leave them without comfort. He would send the Holy Spirit to sustain them and guide them. He had already

If we avoid feeling longing or pain, we will continue to try to fill up our lives with things that leave us hungry.

told them that even though He was leaving this world, He would always abide—live—in them (16:7). And He does the same for us.

On long nights, when worries sit by our beds, on gray days, when we wonder how the clock ticks seamlessly as hours drag on, and on lonely roads, when longing overshadows community, our desire for love does not cease. When I sat vigil by my mother's bed before she died, I thought my heart would break for her. I knew that my youngest children would never get to meet her, I knew she had so much left to give in this world, and I knew I would never love another person like my own mom. I didn't know how to kiss her goodbye as her breathing shallowed and her heart slowed. But what I learned over the course of those hard weeks is that my heart grew in love through that jagged pain. In grieving, hearts can grow stronger, and in pain, there is comfort because love abides.

When You Don't Know Which Way to Go

How sweet are your words to my taste,
    sweeter than honey to my mouth!
I gain understanding from your precepts;
    therefore I hate every wrong path.
Your word is a lamp for my feet,
    a light on my path.

PSALM 119:103–105

Healed Edges

Once, at a weekly meeting with the group of survivors at Thistle Farms, the women all talked about what it meant to heal on the edges of their hearts and expand them. One woman described how for her it meant feeling the heat of summer. When she was in jail and on the streets, she was so far gone that she felt nothing, not even the heat. Now when she felt hot, she acknowledged that even with the sensations others might think unpleasant, she was just grateful to feel them. The woman to her right said this was the first year she had ever seen a chipmunk. She knew that they must have been around her all her life, but after running away as a young teen, she never even noticed them. Her life and faith now were so strong, she said, "I am hearing and seeing things I never knew I was missing."

The stories went on and on. Finally, one woman said, "I think for me, growing in my life and faith has expanded my capacity to feel compassion. Now when I see another woman walking down the streets, I want to help her so bad. I know that she is going through hell on earth. I would say I have never had ups and downs—I have always been down. Now that I'm learning how love heals, I just want to reach back and grab as many other women as I can."

These are just a couple expressions that describe how women feel their hearts expanding as they heal. They take in new sights and feel compassion on what was once the painful edges of their hearts.

The Apostles on Healing

After the death and resurrection of Jesus, a community gathered together in wonder, but they were still struggling to understand what had just happened among them. They had experienced miracles of healing: the lame could walk, the deaf could hear, the blind could see. In the book of Acts, beginning in the third chapter, Peter and John spoke about the deep desire to understand how love had overcome death in the resurrection. After all, these were the people who had shouted, "Hosanna in the highest" when Jesus entered Jerusalem, only to cry out for His crucifixion just days later. They were at a loss, looking to the apostles for an explanation for these mysteries and certainly for help with the pain of confusion they must have felt. Because Peter and John had been witnesses to great love and had been loved greatly, they had compassion for the community that wanted to heal.

In Acts, they spoke to the community in detail, to give them advice on how they should carry on in the face of their brokenness:

1. *Repent of your sins.* Peter invited the crowd to begin their journey of understanding: "Repent, then, and turn to God so that your sins may be wiped out" (Acts 3:19). Part of our pain comes from our own thoughts, words, and deeds. We repent of things we have done and left undone so that we can love again with our whole hearts. When

we experience the freedom rooted in forgiveness, we don't have to block out those places too painful to think about or numb ourselves from the shame of our past.

2. *Remain in fellowship.* Peter knew that for the community *to* grow, they needed to seek out fellowships of faith where they *could* grow. Acts 2:46–47 shows us this principle in action: "Continuing daily with one accord in the temple, and breaking bread from house to house, they ate their food with gladness and simplicity of heart" (NKJV). We can't expand and strengthen our hearts if we stay comfortable where we are. We need to learn a new way to see and act. Communities of faith teach us new ideas about how to live more fully.

3. *Live in generosity.* We give generously because of all the mercy and grace we have been shown. A grateful heart is a healing heart. Acts 4:32 tells us, "All the believers were one in heart and mind. No one claimed that any of their possessions was their own, but they shared everything they had."

4. *Heal one another.* My healing is bound to your healing. I pray for you; you pray for me. The early Christians were concerned that the needs of widows and the sick were cared for, so they selected from amongst themselves "seven men of good standing, full of the Spirit and of wisdom, whom we may appoint to this task" (Acts 6:3 NRSV). The Acts of the Apostles is filled with stories of healing through the

work of the community. Healing love is meant to be shared with one another. Even though we can't fathom the reality of divine love requited, our desire to help others find healing keeps us close to God.

With these four steps in mind, everyone can begin to expand and strengthen their hearts. Peter and John's advice offers us a way to heal through God's Spirit within us—and the desire we have been given to love deeply.

Love Lives Within Us

The lessons we learn from Peter, John, and Jesus remind us that the Love of God lives within us. It is not just that we give and receive love—we *are* love. There are no real edges to our hearts in the eternal relationship with God. If we desire healing, we are invited to examine those broken parts that we can't mask with bandages, ignore by distractions, or cover up with buying more things. Instead, in order to heal, we journey inward. We reflect. We face the pain, knowing that our Lord is with us: "For if our heart condemns us, God is greater than our heart, and knows all things" (1 John 3:20–21 NKJV). Finding these new spaces in our hearts allows us to contemplate the eternal, which "has made everything beautiful in its time. He has also set eternity in the human heart" (Ecclesiastes 3:11).

It is in that raw hollow of our hearts where prayers are drafted, the miracle of forgiveness is formed, and longing is free to roam. Healing is possible when we allow ourselves the gift of wandering in that space, taking in new ideas, and knowing we are safe traveling into our hearts once again.

As we make this internal exploration, we are reminded that mind and body—thought and deed—are inextricably bound to one another. We can't heal one at the expense of the other. Scripture asks us: "Do you not know that your bodies are temples of the Holy Spirit, who is in you, whom you have received from God?" (1 Corinthians 6:19). We can't think our way into healing and destroy the temples that are our bodies, and we can't exercise our way to wholeness without faith, a willingness to change, and inspiration. And we can't do anything without the great Healer. As we commit our bodies and minds toward healing, we can trust that the Holy Spirit will lead us toward wholeness in times when we grow weary or when either our body or mind lets us down. We can dig deep and come face-to-face with what remains unhealed in us because we have faith in the Spirit who loves us.

The deep and abiding love of Jesus sates our longing, quells our fear, and allows us to love others with more courage and generosity. We can love because we are full of love.

Love Pushes Forward

What happens when we face the rough edges and begin to heal? When we make the space to come home to our hearts, we find space to dream and think new thoughts. New ideas come from making room in our hearts through the hard work of reflection and forgiveness. Those new ideas blossom into actions that bring others new life. Beyond our thirst for knowledge and our hunger for justice, we all intrinsically yearn to find new ways to love.

Paul, who grew from a murderer of Christians to the great apostle, said to the whole city of Athens, "The God who made the world and everything in it is the Lord of heaven and earth," has made people "so that they would reach out for him and find him, though he is not far from any one of us" (Acts 17:24, 27). We don't allow weariness, cynicism, or pain to stop us from reaching, grasping for God on the edges of our hearts. We don't allow our past failures to shame us into numbing ourselves. Paul certainly didn't, and look what God did with him.

When we experience a feeling that is unpleasant, we remember that no feeling is final and we sit with it, uncovering more and more until we get to the edges of our hearts, where we realize that the Spirit of God is holding us, living in us, and loving us. And then we fall in love again.

Shelia is a graduate of the residential program of Thistle Farms. She is speaking this year at the United Nations about how love is powerful enough to heal hearts around the world. She describes her life before the community as violent and terrifying. She tells stories of how she was duct-taped and thrown into the Great Salt Lake, of the times when she was beaten so badly that her head split open, and of running away from a murderer when she was still a teenager. It all started in the hills of Tennessee with an addicted mother who used Shelia's body to get the drugs she craved. Shelia never knew security.

After being in the community for several months, she talked to us about what it meant for her to "come home."

An Exercise in Silence

Silent prayer is an ancient, effective way to face the rough edges of our hearts. Find a place to sit and still yourself. Close your eyes and breathe long, deep breaths. You should be able to feel your ribs expand and your belly rise and fall. After about ten minutes or so, you can start to feel like not just your ribs and belly are expanding, but so is your heart. Whatever tenderness, grief, and hope reside in you, you can feel them through a contemplative prayer. When you have said, "Amen," take the peace that passes understanding and the truth you learned from the Holy Spirit and go with a heart grateful to God into the rest of your day.

"*Home*," she said, "is a powerful word to someone who has never felt safe."

When Shelia came home to herself, she found new edges on her heart, and she realized her heart couldn't break. She went through cancer and the death of friends, and she still kept dreaming of sharing her new home with other women. She faced the pain and found strength from a God who loved her with a healing love.

Then she started to find new ways to love. She fell in love with a good man. She had two children, got her degree, and started speaking around the world. The *New York Times* wrote an op-ed piece about her in 2015 called, "From the Streets to the 'World's Best Mom.'" This year she is celebrating ten years of marriage by renewing her vows. I know that when she recommits herself to the love of her life, we will all sit in the congregation and weep. We will weep for all the pain she suffered, all the work she has put in, and how she is still an innocent child of God. Because the rough edges of her heart have been smoothed and healed, she pushes the boundaries of love a little further for all of us.

Whatever tenderness, grief, and hope reside in you, you can feel them through contemplative prayer.

CHAPTER 7

LOVE HEALS IN THE VALLEY OF DEATH

Embracing the grief that connects us

In the Valley of Death

With arms outstretched on the hill

An American chestnut tree stands resurrected.

Silently she draws new life from an old, dead stump

Where her ancestors died with blighted roots a hundred years ago.

She bears witness to the graves lying stoneless in her valley.

The sunken earth is the only marker

For brothers and sisters, enslaved, laid too shallow.

The woodland cemetery is adorned with vine wreathes

Among pawpaws and May apples that keep wake.

People lay down and wept here in the shadow of death.

The rising Chestnut holds this broken history in her belly.

On this sacred ground an owl flies at half-mast and calls out,

"We cannot kill what God calls very good."

Nothing is forsaken since love seeps through

Shallow graves and dead stumps.

We weep for blights and injustices,

But even if we hung up our lyre,

The bluebirds and yellowbellied sapsuckers

Sing for the weary, "There is love after death."

*B*urying those we love is the hardest task of our lives. That is why at gravesides tears flow freely—as deep calls to deep. Those tears are made of the same stuff as the waters that set the captives free in Egypt. Those tears of grief accompany us through the hard and holy ground of returning to God.

The most difficult part is feeling how quickly everything but love returns to dust. Death scares all of us when we contemplate its power, and fear is usually lurking close by. While love cannot immediately remove the sting of death for those who remain, in love death is diminished as we make our song of hope. "Where, O death, is your victory? Where, O death, is your sting?" (1 Corinthians 15:55). Even as we face loss, God gives us clues in the midst of grief that love is with us—and in the end, love is more powerful than death.

Three times since the early death of my father when I was five, an age before my memories could take root, I have dreamed of him: once in college, once at a church convention in 2003, and recently while I slept in the hills of Alabama. He was a pastor, and I have loved carrying on his legacy of serving the church. In the most recent dream, we were together in the room that holds all the supplies for the church services, called the *sacristy*, at Saint Augustine's Chapel in Nashville. There, where I have worked setting up altars for more than twenty years, candlesticks are stored among chalices and robes. In my dream, I picked up two candlesticks from my father's old mission church in Nashville, and he showed me that hidden

There is always more balm to heal than pain to suffer.

inside the candlestick bases were wads of lamb's wool he had stored. Lamb's wool is the traditional fiber ministers use to apply dabs of healing oil when they visit the sick. When I took out the wool, another older man was in the sacristy with us. He had tears welling up in his eyes, and my father gave me permission to take the wool and dry his tears.

My dream was filled with overwhelming grief, but also present was a tenderness and compassion that felt like the balm in Gilead we read and sing about. Even in the face of death, there is healing and hope, the dream reminded me. Gilead was a rocky region east of the Jordan that was home to the people of Israel who grieved and longed for God. When the prophet Jeremiah cried out, "Is there no balm in Gilead? Is there no physician there? Why then is there no healing for the wound of my people?" he knew there was, and his cry was to his people to remember that they had access to it (Jeremiah 8:22). There is always more balm to heal than pain to suffer. We are always in the presence of the Great Physician, who carries us all the way home.

The balm in the wilderness of Gilead offers us new and secret places of healing found tucked beneath the golden candles that mark our altars. Sometimes in the most hurting and haunted places, we are able to discover the great depth of love. In my dream, the healing balm in the lamb's wool, tucked beneath the light, is compassion bestowed with a fearless love for all those who are grieving. It makes sense to me that the bearer of the healing wool was my father, from whom the only line of preaching I know of is on a slip of paper I found tucked in his Bible that read, "In the shadow of his cross may your soul find rest." We are called to love and heal in the midst of the shadows of our own grieving. Whether we are talking about the suffering of death of someone we love or the general grief experienced from war, disease, or oppression, we are called to look beneath the golden candles to discover new healing.

A Promise from Jesus When Healing Seems Far Away:

"Come to me, all you who are weary and burdened, and I will give you rest. Take my yoke upon you and learn from me, for I am gentle and humble in heart, and you will find rest for your souls. For my yoke is easy and my burden is light."

MATTHEW 11:28–30

The Balm of Hope

On one of my annual pilgrimages to Ecuador, I hiked up into the Andes to a waterfall at what felt like the top of the world. It is a place so high that each breath is deep and your mind is in the heavens. The water smells like clouds rushing to get to the river. I was silenced by the magnitude and power of that water. While I was standing there, the waterfall tossed a huge volcanic boulder like a skipping stone. There on that transfiguring mountaintop, I wept at the majesty of the waterfall and thought about all the time I've wasted in my life wondering how the stone was really rolled away from Jesus' tomb on Easter morning. I could see, standing there, how easily stones can be moved.

Water can move rocks, and thistles can break through boulders to bloom. If water and flowers can move stones, surely love can. In death there is a deluge of love like rushing water. It clears out everything to make room for a soul that has been set free. In that deluge, the stones of our hearts and in front of tombs are rolled away, time and eternity meet, and we are laid to rest in the bosom of Abraham. This means we can trust that the love we have known in this world will carry us home to God. Nothing can compare to the hope of resurrection. It is what sets us free and allows love to heal throughout our lives.

A Poem for Hope in Healing

A bluebird whistled a tune on a magnolia blossom
As a hawk cut through the lavender sky.
Old tulip trees danced
As mountains broke into song.
Squirrels danced on a wire
As flowers opened in unison.
Just as Jesus broke our hearts wide open,
the stone that kept hope at bay
finally rolled away.

The Balm of Gratitude

I am amazed by the power of grief. One of my most startling lessons about grief came long after we buried my father, and later my mother and sister—not to mention the many women in the community of Thistle Farms, the congregants, and even the strangers I have laid to rest. It came while I was on vacation. A house sitter called to say that Goldie, the goldfish my youngest son and I had won at a state fair about nine months before, had died. Goldie was silent in her water world, and for almost a year I had been mindful of her needs amid all the noise in my life. Just before I put my son to bed, the last thing we did was feed Goldie and make sure her tank was clean. I couldn't believe I was grieving her, but I couldn't help it.

Her death marked the end of the sweet time when snuggling my youngest boy and watching the fish grow passed like sand in my hand. But I was so grateful for that time. That fish taught me to be grateful in grief—but also that we don't get to choose what we grieve. We can grieve getting pregnant; we can grieve not getting pregnant. We can grieve a relationship that has been broken and relationships we never even had. We can grieve anything our hearts have been sweet on, and it is released when we say goodbye to what we hold dear. Grief, like gratitude, is a universal language we recognize in others because each person's grief is related to our own. We all carry grief as part of our story. Yet in order to live well and free, we need gratitude, even in the face of death. With gratitude, healing is not abandoned in death; it is completed. And as we breathe our last breath on this planet, we need to leave grateful.

The Balm of Humility

Love heals through the valley of death, too, because it teaches us humility. Death reminds us not to take anything for granted, not even our next breath. It keeps us focused on building not only résumés but also legacies that preach love. The temporal nature of our lives gives us a chance to experience humility as a spiritual practice.

One way to practice this humility is to think about how much of what you have has been a gift from others. Think about how so much of what we think will last forever . . . passes. Then think about how you will leave this earth with nothing but the legacy of love you have left. It doesn't take long to get humble and grateful.

The Benedictine rule of the fourteenth century teaches us, as passing pilgrims, to have a reverence for God, to endure affliction, to be obedient, and to feel content. Monastic communities in the seventeenth century taught followers to have a right opinion of themselves, to let go of pride, to practice contentment, and even to give thanks for weaknesses. This is one example of a spiritual disciplines aimed at making us humble, grateful, and faithful. We are just passing through this world; our faith asks us to hope, be grateful, grieve, and live with humility.

As we heal in the valley of death, we surrender our lives to God in humility, follow the path before us, and proclaim without fear that we can trust God with our lives. We can trust that God will carry us to the eternal side of time despite our fears of death and dying for ourselves and others. No matter what, we will never be forgotten by our Creator, who reminds us we are more valuable than sparrows (Matthew 10:29).

To say that we are more valuable than a humble sparrow is actually saying something powerful. Sparrows, though common and somewhat plain, are skillful fliers, darting with strength and moving with grace. They are resilient and have a bloodline that carries them back to the days of Scripture. They are mesmerizing to watch, have beautiful babies, and can sing the glory of every morning. To be loved even as much as a humble sparrow is lavish, and it gives me comfort. We can all look at the birds of the air and remember our belovedness.

※

Sometimes we get glimpses of heaven, like when we're standing under a waterfall on top of the world, or when we dream of those who have died. Sometimes we are humbled by all we have to grieve—even our pets. But never are we left without glimpses of what eternity must be like.

Heaven is like the memory of God. All of us are preserved in the memory of God, which is big enough to contain all creation for all time. Nothing can erase us from the memory of God, and no one on this earth is forgotten. That same passage from Matthew 6:26 that asks us to consider the birds of the air and the grasses of the field reminds us that we will never be forgotten by God, not even the Jane Does who have died alone in a world where no one knew their names. So when we move beyond all our individual and collective fears about death and being forgotten in this world, we move into a deeper place of love where we live fuller lives for all the days we are graced to live.

Death can teach us about humility, gratitude, and hope. But as much as it might sting, it doesn't stop the beauty of the flight of a sparrow or the touch of lamb's wool. Death doesn't get the last word; love does. Before there was death, there was love.

CHAPTER 8

LOVE HEALS ON THE MOUNTAINTOP

Seeking God's inspiration

Up on the Mountaintop

The storm is brewing in the mountaintop.

Clouds become a stage for lightning dances.

Thunder rolls in a distant heaven.

Soaring above, predators scan meadows

For the most vulnerable prey,

Like I am searching the horizon for a thought.

Moses saw God alongside hawks gliding on updrafts,

Carrying lofty thoughts

Where longings are sated by inspiration.

Mountaintops roar with power.

Born in the depths of sea,

They are the survivors.

We climb their stoic backs,

Hoping like the hawks and Moses

to dwell with mountain dreams.

While mountaintops are coveted spots, climbing up to them is a physical, mental, and emotional challenge. It takes courage to climb the mountains on our faith journey—especially after spending time low in the valley. Spiritually, "mountaintops" are experiences where we feel like we are soaring in the heavens like eagles. They are high points where we feel transcended by the Holy Spirit, enfolded in the arms of God, or like we can see a vision of God's kingdom. Sometimes love swoops in during unexpected moments of transformation in mountaintop experiences, but before and after those moments, planning and hard work are required. Experiencing these inspired moments and heavenly visions can lead to healing—and like healing, they are found over time with effort and focus.

When Jesus, Peter, James, and John went to the mountaintop to experience Jesus' transfiguration—where they saw Him in dazzling white standing with Moses and Elijah—they had already been working in the mission field for a couple years. Jesus' cousin John the Baptist had already been imprisoned and executed. They had already watched Jesus feed and cure thousands, teach in parables, calm the sea, and confront the religious authorities in the synagogues. They didn't just wander up to that mountain out of nowhere. That moment followed hard work, disciplined prayer, and lives given in their mission.

Jesus led them, "up a high mountain . . . [and] he was transfigured before them. His face shone like the sun, and his clothes became as white as the light" (Matthew 17:1–2). As Elijah and Moses joined Him, it was like heaven appeared on earth. The hard work and prayer equipped the disciples to climb the mountain and experience that transfiguring moment when Jesus stood with the ancient prophets. And even with that work, it was still hard for them to fathom such a powerful transfiguration. They were terrified by what they had seen, and in their fear, they wanted to do something practical—to put up shelter that clearly wasn't needed. So Jesus needed to reach out and touch them and say, "Get up . . . Don't be afraid" before they prepared, heads down and with their eyes on Jerusalem, to meet the work ahead (v. 7).

Moses, too, spent years in preparation for his mountaintop: the moment on Mount Sinai when he was given the Ten Commandments. He had walked on sacred ground, released the captives in Egypt, and wandered in the wilderness for years. Finally, when he was alone on the mountaintop, God spoke to him: "There is a place near me where you may stand on a rock. When my glory passes by, I will put you in a cleft in the rock and cover you with my hand until I have passed by. Then I will remove my hand and you will see my back" (Exodus 33:21–23). The Scripture then says that after this, Moses obeyed by carving out the commandments and then bowed his head and worshiped.

Since the days of Moses, pilgrims have been going to the mountaintop to retreat and to find answers, peace, and healing. Once, in the middle of an Ecuador trip to serve a community of women there, I happened to climb an actual mountain as a fog rolled in. It was in the rain forest, and I had no idea how high we were or where the steep edge of the path was. I was tired by the time I reached the top and sat to catch my breath and close my eyes. I could see the light changing through my closed lids, and it looked like prisms dancing through the dark. I opened my eyes as I took another breath and realized the sun had come out. I saw a breathtaking vista of thick forest floor, gleaming in a thousand shades of green. I felt like I was in heaven, and immediately my eyes welled up. I was overjoyed and felt at peace. It felt as holy as if I could have been with Moses as God's glory passed by, or with Peter, James, and John as the Lord's clothes were illuminated.

I believe we do the majority of our work in the valley. A mountaintop experience is a rare and glorious surprise that we prepare for by taking all the steps laid out in the previous chapters. You will know when you have reached a climactic moment on your journey when you experience inexpressible joy and clarity. It will renew your heart and give you the energy to keep walking back in the valley for a long while. The mountaintop heals us. It is where we can see great vistas and experience the euphoric feeling of standing in the clouds. We remember the psalmist, who wrote, "I lift up my eyes to the mountains—where does my help come from? My help comes from the LORD, the Maker of heaven and earth" (Psalm 121:1–2).

The mountaintop is where the heavens and earth meet and where we feel lighter than the air we are breathing, where we are inspired to think new thoughts. It is where we go to retreat, and it is where vision is born.

I believe there are four steps on this journey to the mountaintop where love's healing power awaits.

A Prayer of Joy

Let the sun set in bands of orange and pink.

Let the waves move like an alleluia choir.

Let the dandelions scatter confetti seeds in celebration.

Let the moon smile as it wanes.

Let the children's songs be heard.

Let my heart feel the joy it was meant to hold.

Amen.

Step 1: Pack Wisely

Ask yourself what you need to let go of to make the long, steep climb toward close communion with God. If you take too much baggage, you will fall under the weight of it. The thin air and the push of the earth will make you feel like you can't catch your breath. To climb, we have to travel light. It is the first thing Jesus told the disciples as they were commissioned in Matthew's gospel: "Do not [take] any gold or silver or copper . . . in your belts—no bag for the journey or extra

Leave behind the chip on your shoulder, the old resentments, the critical thoughts, and the fears that keep you feeling stuck and unable to climb.

shirt or sandals or a staff" (10:9–10). I would add: leave behind the chip on your shoulder, the old resentments, the critical thoughts, and the fears that keep you feeling stuck and unable to climb.

One of the women at Thistle Farms once said that in order for her to make the climb out of the gutters of street survival to living in a home, she had to drop her cell phone. It was so thin and small, yet it was so heavy. In that phone was her past—filled with the names of drug dealers and men who had bought her. As long as she held on to that small, thin phone, she was going to be trapped on the streets forever. When she let go, she could climb to a place with a beautiful view, where she could hear the birds sing and notice the glory of the changing seasons.

Step 2: Plan for Mishaps

Prepare for hardships you may encounter. That way when there is a rustling in the bushes, you won't react like it's a man-eating animal when it's just a squirrel. For example, when we started planning a program with women refugees from the Syrian war, we met obstacle after obstacle. We had a plan, and we didn't bolt at the first problem. Having the plan allowed us to travel to Greece and watch the healing journey of the first women's enterprise in the refugee camp unfold. We don't want to bolt at the first thunderstorm, unfamiliar sound, or blocked path. If fear holds us back from seeking our healing, we need a plan to meet those fears and obstacles that will crop up. Jesus told His disciples that when they encountered hostility, they should wipe the dust from their feet and keep going (Matthew 10:14). Chances are that the problems you fear you will meet are bound up in shame. To combat the shame, make your pilgrim's plan with people you trust, people who can help you make the climb. This could be a support group from church, a close group of sisters or brothers you meet with weekly, or a family member or friend. These are the people who are willing to stick by you when times are rough, who will keep encouraging you to seek, know, and ask your way toward the mountaintop. Joining together with these people is part of the journey to get to the mountaintop.

Step 3: Enjoy the Storms

Learn to see hardships and obstacles on the climb as part of the healing journey. Those storms and wild animals make our hearts race, make all our senses awaken, make us pray exactly what is on our hearts. I have forgotten so many of the hikes I've made over the years, but I have never forgotten the walk where I met a bear, or almost stepped on a snake, or walked through thunderous clouds pelting me with rain.

I remember vividly one morning years ago, when I was taking a hike and the weather turned. I was the only person on the trail, and although it was morning, the low light made it feel like evening. Everything was shades of gray. I glanced to my right where the rocky ledge overlooked a lake, and there was a bald eagle sitting next to me. The fog was thick enough that the eagle may not have seen me. I stood with the eagle and watched the lake with him. I felt like Isaiah, who must have been writing from a place with a view when he said, "Those who hope in the LORD will renew their strength. They will soar on wings like eagles; they will run and not grow weary" (Isaiah 40:31). I felt more energy and joy on that walk than I ever could have found staying home. We will encounter storms, but if we recognize them as a necessary part of the climb, they hold great gifts for us—gifts like God's glory, inspiration, and transformation.

Step 4: Give Thanks

When you finally get there—when you feel God's presence and healing love around you—allow yourself to let the moment on the mountaintop sink deep into your heart. Take time to thank God with all your heart for the moments of grace when you feel joy. Thank God for all the moments that led to your feeling whole, healed, and inspired. Thank God for all the people who helped you get there, for every kind deed done and left undone to you, for every ounce of forgiveness. Find gratitude even for all the hearts you broke or those who broke yours to help you get there and for everything you may have forgotten. I have led too many mission trips where the grace of the work gets lost because we forgot to let it sink deep into our hearts and transform us. We get so busy in the doing that we forget that part of the journey is to reflect and feel transformed by the work.

Getting perspective on the huge gift of mountaintop experiences means we are willing to stop and reflect. Giving thanks brings the full gift of the moment to light and lets it shine deep within our hearts.

The promise we are given in faith is that all those who seek, find—which means all of those searching for the mountaintop can find the way to get there. That is a deep and abiding hope that can carry us a long way on the path to healing.

> I will sing to the Lord,
> for he is highly exalted.
> Both horse and driver
> he has hurled into the sea.
> The Lord is my strength and my defense;
> he has become my salvation.
> He is my God, and I will praise him,
> my father's God, and I will exalt him.
>
> Exodus 15:1–2

CHAPTER 9

LOVE HEALS BY THE MERCY OF GOD

*Accepting God's greatest
gift in gratitude*

The Cherry Tree

There was a day when I was so broken,
I felt like the abandoned kitten I'd found
On the side of an old county road
With flies feasting on his fleshy wound.
You found me in a grieving state
knowing there were no words to be said.
You gave your shoulder for my head,
Where I could weep an ocean.
Then you dug a hole in my front yard,
Planting a sapling from your family's old farm.
It wasn't any taller than my knee,
A beautiful, flowering cherry tree.
Over twenty tree rings and counting,
Inconsolable grief now memory.
Through freezing winters and silent droughts,
The tree grew steady with strong silky leaves.
Mercy is more than twice blessed,
Like thousands of cherries from a single tree.
In giving it you blessed my children,
Hungry cardinals, brazen squirrels, and me.

A Prayer for Mercy

In Your spirit of mercy, as solid as the ground upon which we make our stand, help us recall when we were hungry, afraid, sick, or imprisoned by bonds and burdens. May that mercy be forged into compassion that loves the whole world without judgment. Forgive us again when we fail to show mercy or come into Your temple for solace and not for strength. Pardon our blindness when we didn't see You in the person we called our enemy. Help us let go of tired bitterness passed on by generations who forgot the freedom of forgiveness. Unite us in the truth that love is the most powerful force for change, and teach us to preach love in action. Lord, in Your mercy, hear our prayer. Amen.

My sister, who has a doctorate in health and human performance, has spent her career developing protocols and tools to help people with spinal cord injuries learn to walk. If you ask her about the single best thing people can use to help their healing, she will say, "Hope." If you ask her what the biggest barrier to healing is, she will say, "Despair." We would all despair without God's mercy—and there would be no hope. *Mercy* is the quality that allows us to hope and heal. Beyond all other spiritual gifts, beyond justice and past our sweat and tears, mercy is the gift that carries us from wilderness to gentle pastures.

No one is too good or too bad to receive mercy. It is offered to us by our God, who is rich in mercy and offers it to us out of great love and compassion (Ephesians 2:4). It is not because of anything we have done. It is simply a gift. Jesus reminds us that God makes the sun rise on the evil and the good and sends rain down on the righteous and the unrighteous (Matthew 5:45). Beyond justice, mercy lives—and when mercy is alive, there is hope, even in places that once felt dead. We may cry out for justice, we may pray for forgiveness, but with mercy we weep—because, by its very nature, it is such a humbling and holy word.

> **Be merciful, just as your Father is merciful.**
>
> *Luke 6:36*

About fourteen years ago, a woman was arrested for the murder of a man who was a drug dealer she worked for on the streets, who had beaten and shot her in the past. She was homeless and addicted, with a criminal record that reached back to when she was first on the streets at thirteen years old. I met her shortly after this arrest and before her trial. You would expect that she wouldn't have been given any mercy— that she would be tried and sent away like so many of the women in prison who were victims long before they were criminals. But instead the judge let her out of jail to come (with an electronic bracelet) into the Thistle Farms community.

This woman, Tracey, stayed on probation for ten years, and during that time, she won back custody of her children and became one of the directors of Thistle Farms. Tracey talks about coming from jail into that home as the greatest experience of mercy she has ever known. Last summer she married the love of her life, with her daughters and granddaughter joining her at the altar in a fairytale wedding with pearl drops and layers of crinoline. Everyone wept as she walked with such grace down the aisle. We wept because it could have gone a very different way. We wept because we were so grateful and Tracey was so beautiful. We wept because we remembered how mercy came our way and we were all blessed because of it.

We may not remember how we have been shown mercy in such a dramatic way, but we all have experiences of it, experiences where we didn't get what we deserved but were offered mercy in what feels like grace wrapped in forgiveness tied up with a bit of luck. Mercy feels like when you are almost broken and a friend picks up the pieces. Mercy is as precious as when you think you can't pay your bills at the end of the month and you find money in your pocket. And mercy is as tender as when you are grieving and find an old note and feel the presence of the one you long for.

Recycling Mercy

To be on the receiving end of God's mercy can cause our tears of joy to overflow, bring us to our knees, and leave us with a grateful heart. In the story of the lepers in the Luke 17, Jesus shows mercy on ten lepers by healing them from their terrible disease. One of the ten comes back to give thanks for the miracle. Jesus asks the leper who has returned, "Where are the other nine?" and then tells the newly healed leper to "Rise and go; your faith has made you well," (vv. 17, 19). This is the crux of the matter in mercy. God may heal us, but to be truly made well, we need to accept that healing and express gratitude for the mercy we have been shown. Otherwise, we may continue to run from our past even though we have been given a reprieve.

One of my old theology teachers, Dr. Ed Farley, describes in his book *Divine Empathy* how we understand love from our experience of stepping into God's field of mercy. There, we learn compassion for others and how gratitude after mercy makes us well. Mercy removes our blinders of ego and allows us to be healed. We don't receive because we performed well or we were deserving. In mercy we know that we don't deserve the healing we experience. No one is too good or not good enough to experience the mercy of God. When we let our egos or fear keep us from praying and receiving mercy, we are missing out on one of God's greatest gifts available to us. We can find mercy wherever we are, even if we feel like a leper outside the gates.

It is because of mercy that we still hope for tomorrow.

Like the healed leper, like the person with the spinal cord injury trying to walk, or like Tracey freed from jail, we can feel the amazing, healing power of mercy. In turn, we can feel gratitude and offer mercy to those around us. The lesson is pretty simple: err on the side of mercy in your attitude toward yourself and others. For practical purposes, the next time you feel judgmental toward someone, try switching to mercy instead. Imagine how that person needs mercy. You, who have been given so much, can be the person who demonstrates mercy by offering a hand, by saying something kind, by giving something that person truly needs.

The journey of healing is not Pollyanna-ish. People go through real injustices, crises, and diseases. They get caught in the crosshairs of war and the losing end of broken relationships. They get fired, or sick, or hurt in accidents, or fall victim to the million other chances and changes of the world that make us feel so tender. In all of these unfolding events, mercy will make the difference. It is because of mercy that we still hope for tomorrow.

Memories of Mercy

When we remember our past, it doesn't take us long to think of times when God showed us mercy, whether in our circumstances or through other people. Mercy in hindsight is clearer. Sometimes while we are

No one is too good or too bad to receive mercy.

experiencing it, we are too broken or lost to take it in. In my own journey of healing, in the private space where I know myself better than anyone, I remember God's mercy vividly. I can remember simple things like teachers giving me a bit of extra time on an assignment or more dramatic moments like when I had a near miss with the law when I was young and foolish. I remember times when I felt like grace was out of reach but during which I was healed. When Thistle Farms was a young organization and I was new at raising money, I got into trouble with bills coming in while the bank accounts were dry. I went to a fellow pastor, who could have scolded me or told me it was my own fault. Instead he asked, "How much money do you need to get through the month?" He showed me mercy, and I will never forget him.

Even in the most painful times, I can remember all the gifts that came my way in the form of a friend, a book, a tree, an answered prayer, room to breathe, or family. I am so grateful that I didn't miss these or stay down in all the times I fell down. Love comes in and dusts us off. Despite all my mess-ups and all the mess-ups of people in our community and all your mess-ups—there is always mercy. There is always hope.

A Prayer When We Feel Vulnerable

Compassionate God, speak to me in whispers and sweet silence.
This day has left me so tender a breeze could break my heart.

Be present as I take my rest, and visit me with kind angels.

In my resting, strengthen my desire for courage.

Enkindle my heart to face the worries of a new day.

Inspire me with a new thought to carry me through.

Renew a right spirit within me to fight injustice.

Let my tears be a sign of compassion, not weariness.

Let my grief be a sign of my love, not my despair.

You are the Holy One who knows that in my weakness,

I find Your strength.

Amen.

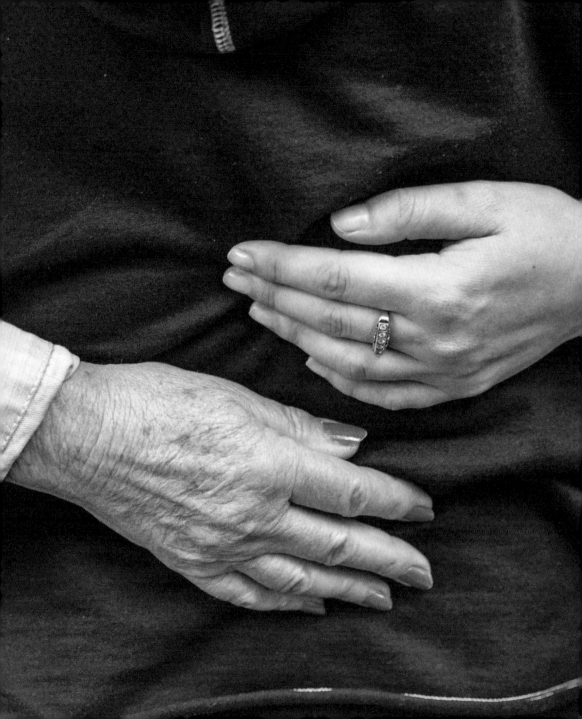

CHAPTER 10

LOVE HEALS DURING THE ACT OF FORGIVING

Transforming brokenness so we can live free

Pearls of Great Price

When I still spoke as a child
And dreamed of being a dancer,
My innocence was traded
For a precious, secret pearl.
I placed it in a silken purse
Bound to my heart for years,
Praying a moth would eat through it
Or a thief cut it loose.
Instead of dancing,
I dreamed of forgiveness
That would let me offer the pearl
More valuable than a widow's mite.
I could lay it on the altar of my youth,
Watching as the stone rolled away.
Then burn the purse as a sign of grace,
dance around the flame.
Marveling at my unbridled heart,
Done grieving things I can't change
While holding on to useless treasure,
I would be free at last.

When we forgive, we can find freedom. When we are free, healing is possible. When we cease to hold on to things that make us sick, we get better. After we accept God's mercy, we feel freer to forgive and let go.

Imagine that you are carrying around all the weight of resentments, bitterness, anger, and regret. Then imagine that freedom is just miles away, and all you have to do to find it is walk there. You can't make it with all the things you haven't forgiven holding you down. Forgiveness means dropping all that weight and walking toward the sweet freedom ahead.

In the Gospels, Jesus teaches us that no matter what, no matter how many times or how hard it is, we need to forgive. When Peter asked Him, "How many times shall I forgive?" Jesus gave him a number big enough that it would take Peter the rest of his life to achieve: seventy times seven (Matthew 18:21–22 NLT). That is how much Jesus wanted Peter to be free.

Forgiving Others

Forgiveness doesn't mean that we forget or that we don't hold one another accountable. It means that we can pray for the other person without sarcasm in our hearts and that we no longer think of the one who has wronged us as our enemy. This, like most of the way of healing, is easier said than done.

I learned this lesson through the act of forgiving the man who abused me for years as a child. He was part of the leadership of the church my father had pastored, and the abuse started after my father's death, when I was about five. Holding on to that secret and feeling angry made me pretty sick. I felt scared and acted out in ways that I later wished I hadn't. I experienced anxiety around authority, thought I needed to prove my worth, and had significant abandonment stress. Even as an adult, I was still suffering the effects of this abuse. Finally, when my oldest son turned five (almost the same age when it all started for me), I knew that if I wanted to be well and serve my children and my community, I needed to be about the business of getting stronger. And that started with forgiving my abuser. It took time and a lot of soul-searching. It didn't happen in a moment, but it did happen when I made the decision not to hold on to it any longer.

The first thing I did was talk to some trusted friends and my husband. Then I talked with a counselor. I began to earnestly pray for the man and his family and myself. I started seeing what had transpired more than two decades earlier differently. I began to see that everyone in the story needed some mercy, and that, in fact, the hard lessons I learned through that trauma had given me a gift of compassion for women on the streets and in prisons.

The next thing I did was difficult and exhausting: I went to this man and his wife and shared my story. My main goal was to give the story of his abuse back to him so I didn't have to carry it like a secret cancer anymore. I wanted them to deal with it. I was very specific and careful in the meeting,

I knew if I wanted to be well and serve my children and my community, I needed to be about the business of getting stronger. And that started with forgiving.

and it was a huge step in learning to forgive. The step of confronting an abuser is not appropriate for everyone; you need to talk with a counselor, pastor, or trusted friend before you embark on such a journey. Sometimes the confrontation can happen through writing, through a mediator, or even in a letter that you write and then burn. Sometimes the abuser has died; sometimes the contact can do more damage than good. For me, it was important to share the story and have a witness to the story. After I confronted my abuser, I wasn't instantly healed. But somewhere along the way, I forgave him. The steps were not linear, and I can't pinpoint when it happened. What I know is that in the act of forgiving, drops of freedom began to seep through the dry ground of my heart, and it turned back into a place where something could grow.

In forgiveness, the small drops of freedom make their way into rivers that allow the healing hope of justice to flow. Without forgiveness, those waters are dry and we are left parched. This world needs more forgiveness for those waters to flow. Without forgiveness the waters of faith are in a drought.

A Vision of Healing

But now, this is what the Lord says—
he who created you, Jacob,
he who formed you, Israel:

"Do not fear, for I have redeemed you;

I have summoned you by name; you are mine.

When you pass through the waters,

I will be with you;

and when you pass through the rivers,

they will not sweep over you.

When you walk through the fire,

you will not be burned;

the flames will not set you ablaze.

For I am the LORD your God,

the Holy One of Israel, your Savior;

I give Egypt for your ransom,

Cush and Seba in your stead.

[You] are precious and honored in my sight,

and because I love you."

ISAIAH 43:1–4

Forgiving Ourselves

We are here to love ourselves, each other, and God (Mark 12:30–31). But in order to love ourselves—and love our neighbors—we need to forgive ourselves. Forgiving ourselves is one of the hardest parts of living free and well. We know what our secrets are; we know everything we have done and everything we have left undone. When we can't forgive ourselves, we stay sick, and those things keep us living in shame.

I'm reminded of the day I was sitting on a bench outside with a woman in the Thistle Farms community. She began to weep; I hadn't said a word. Then she started talking about how she just didn't get it. She got that people loved her. She got that her faith told her she was forgiven. She got that she needed to grow in this community so she could live into her full potential. What she said she couldn't get was how to forgive herself.

"What can't you forgive?" I asked her. The sobs grew, and she started sharing a litany of her wrongs from about the age of twelve until she was thirty. It was some hard and bad baggage to carry, but for whatever reason on that particular day, she was done with it. She was ready to confess it in a safe place and see if she could find healing.

As I listened, I didn't go through each of her wrongs and parse them out. I just held the story for her and kept saying silent prayers for her to find the faith to forgive herself so she could love herself. She will have time to make restitution and to discover how she was a victim long before she was a criminal. She will have a great therapist to help her figure out how to work through it all, whether through talking, writing, painting, or something else. She will have a community to pray with her and to help her find solace in the Scriptures. All she needed before she began was someone to hear her story and still love her.

Those are the times I feel most grateful for all I have learned about forgiveness. Once we have forgiven ourselves, then stories that may have been hard for us to hear are now an opportunity to show compassion for a sister.

That feels like motivation enough for all of us to start working on forgiving ourselves. Whether you can find a safe place to share the worst or if you need to confess it all to God, letting your burdens pour out and taking them off your heart will free you.

Freedom in Forgiveness

The freedom we find in forgiveness is not idealistic imagining. The freedom found in forgiving ourselves and others is an axiom of faith sung by psalmists and touted by prophets. Prophets like Micah forgave much and were given blessings and freedom as a result.

> Who is a God like You,
> Pardoning iniquity
> And passing over the transgression of the remnant of His
>   heritage?
> He does not retain His anger forever,
> Because He delights in mercy.
> He will again have compassion on us,

And will subdue our iniquities.
You will cast all our sins
Into the depths of the sea.

MICAH 7:18–19 NKJV

Learning the art of forgiveness is a daily practice, like the other means of healing love we've talked about in this book. Like anything else, we become better at forgiving as we devote ourselves to it intentionally. Forgiveness is something we need to *practice*. We need to practice it in the woods, in prison, in church, at work, and at home. If we can't forgive, we

When we forgive, we can find freedom. When we are free, healing is possible.

must practice harder, or change the practice of our faith. Faith is rooted in God's forgiveness and in our ability to forgive each other and ourselves. That is the way we will find the keys to the kingdom.

Today, give a few of these a try as you work to forgive yourself and others.

1. Decide one thing you need to forgive.
2. Pray for the thing (or person) that holds you in bondage.
3. Take a practical step that will help you to forgive, such as writing a letter or setting up a time to talk to a pastor or counselor.

4. Imagine what it might be like to have forgiven that person or thing.

5. Picture what amends (atoning) might look like for you to feel forgiven or to forgive.

6. Pray again for the obstacles holding you back from forgiving yourself or others.

7. Start again the next day.

Then practice these seven steps seventy more times.

CHAPTER 11

LOVE HEALS FROM PAST MISTAKES

Letting go of what weighs us down

Tripped Up

I cross my heart at the altar,
then trip over my own two feet.
I get in my way so easily
that roots, open doors, or tiny cracks
throw me for a loop.
Walking with grace is a dream
Offered to flawless women I pass.
I know my mistakes so well.
They are scarred on the back of my hand,
tattooed on my lower back,
and etched on my heart.
I wonder if people see them in my eyes
or read them into every line
I write about mercy.
The times I have tripped
Kept me close to the ground.
Mistakes have taught me everything
I have ever known about love.
My missteps lead me to the place
Where I can trust that
Tripping puts me into love's arms.

We all stumble, but past mistakes shouldn't keep us from moving forward on the journey of healing. In fact, mistakes hold valuable lessons for us to heed. There is no shame in making mistakes; the problem occurs if we don't learn from them. After we've done the work of accepting mercy from God, forgiving others, and forgiving ourselves, it's time to embark on the separate but all-important process of learning from the gifts of our mistakes and making amends. Scripture teaches us to recognize our mistakes, learn from them, and not let them keep us broken. I love the psalmist's cry: "Though he may stumble, he will not fall, for the LORD upholds him with his hand" (Psalm 37:24). We stumble, but that is not the end of the journey. We are still being upheld by a loving hand. Mistakes are the reason there has always been and always will be a need for prophets to call to us from the wilderness, that we should repent and make a straight path through the desert (Isaiah 40:3).

In the community of Thistle Farms, we believe that in every mistake, there is potential for healing. Nothing a person can do will close the door forever with God and with a loving community—even if that person feels beyond redemption, is put back in prison, or cannot find sobriety in this life. Our practice is simple: take a step back, apologize, make amends, learn something new, and move on.

One woman had been in our community for about a year when she went back into a dangerous relationship and relapsed. She broke hearts in the community, borrowed money she was never going to pay back, stole items from friends, and lied. The damage was like a tsunami with a wake of destruction that made her relationships seem unsalvageable. She ended up back in prison. Still, sisters from the Thistle Farms community reached out to her and kept reminding her that there is always a *bottom*—the word describing the worst it can get. But once you have hit it, you can start climbing your way out. She has continued to work hard in prison and is learning from her mistakes. She is helping convene groups for women in recovery, she is writing letters, and she has apologized. Over the past few years, she has reached out and helped some new women find recovery and make their way toward Thistle Farms upon their release. While she still has years in prison to learn from her mistakes and build a bridge to pass over the troubled waters she stirred up, she may yet make it home. Her mistakes, which were many, do not mean she can't heal or help others find healing.

> *There is always a* bottom—*the word describing the worst it can get. But once you have hit it, you can start climbing your way out.*

Again, learning from our past mistakes includes the important lessons described in the chapters on mercy and forgiveness. When we learn from rather than run from our past, it can actually become a powerful part of our healing story. Even the mistakes and brokenness become part of the good news. This woman's story is descended from the beautiful story in the seventh chapter of Luke's gospel, where a woman from the streets came into the circle of disciples and poured perfumed oil over Jesus' feet. As she wept, she kissed His feet and wiped them with her hair. Jesus defended her actions, saying her sins were forgiven because she had shown great love. He explained the story's meaning by comparing our mistakes to a person with a debt to pay. The bigger the debt or the bigger the mistake, the bigger the chance to love greatly. "Therefore, I tell you, her many sins have been forgiven—as her great love has shown. But whoever has been forgiven little loves little" (v. 47). Our past mistakes may become the very foundation upon which we learn that great love is possible.

The woman came in with a gift of oils in an expensive jar. She knew her offering needed to be a lavish outpouring to represent her gratitude for the priceless gift of freedom and forgiveness. Who knows how long she had been stuck on the streets? Who knows the humiliation and violence she had suffered while there, and who knows what she had done to keep herself alive? But Jesus gave her permission to move forward—free at last from past mistakes.

In this story, we can see that the healing that comes from forgiveness of our mistakes is both lavish and messy. Imagine this woman as she poured the ointment out and let her hair fall into the mess. Imagine the spill on the floor and the awkward moment as she tried to wipe up the oils cascading over Jesus' feet and over their garments and onto the floor of the Pharisee's house—all with her own hair. Making amends for our past mistakes can be messy, but it is the way we get better. Healing is always possible.

For Thistle Farms, this story means that, in making amends, the brokenness, harm, or shame of our past is transformed into something holy. That feels miraculous to me. It's not in spite of our past; it is because of our past that we are made whole.

Moving Forward in Faith

Making amends may be as simple as saying, "I'm sorry" or paying restitution. It can be as big as knowing you need to change something radically. Because making amends can be messy, there are tried-and-true principles to hold on to as you move through. These are the steps Thistle Farms uses to learn from mistakes.

1. Take a Step Back

All of us wish we could backtrack and start over from time to time. How did we get to the point where we want to press the reset button? If we are to learn from mistakes, we'll need to know how and why we made them. Retracing our steps can be a gift—it helps us remember who we are and where we come from. This means spending time in reflection to see where we may have taken a wrong turn. It also may include hearing other people's version of events surrounding our mistakes. The healing path is not always straight, and it's usually not easy. When we feel like we have

The bigger the debt or the bigger the mistake, the bigger the chance to love greatly.

circled back around to a place we've been before, we get to take a closer look at where we have been and recognize what we need to do to move forward. As we retrace our steps, sometimes we find ourselves again, and we learn how to love better and what it means to pour out our best oils to soothe others' suffering. Our own mistakes, which are many, give us the tools we need to love greatly.

2. Apologize

Sometimes it feels like my mistakes are too big for even a beautiful jar of oil to wipe away, no matter how lavish it is. The lavish oil in this story represents how costly, precious, and messy apologizing and asking for forgiveness can be. When we worry that our past mistakes are just too big, change seems impossible. That is when we most need to gather our precious gifts, retrace our steps, and pour out the oil for the sake of love. That is when we finally remember that "love heals" is not just a truth reserved for others; it is also a truth for ourselves.

A Prayer for Guidance

Anoint my head with the balm of peace, and set me on the right path. Give me courage to get back up when I stumble. Give me the eyes to see Your hand at work in the world around me. Teach me to pray for others even in my own suffering. Show me how to love again from the deepest part of my heart and with my whole being. Amen.

3. Make Amends

No mistake, no matter how grave it feels, can keep love from doing the work of healing. Love grows exponentially as it is poured out, and it can cover a multitude of mistakes. When we trip up, we have the tools to express great love and to humble ourselves through lavish and messy acts of amends—and to get up and try again. A good backslide lands us on our backsides every now and then! But it also lets us get close to the earth and allows us to see how love dusts off our knees. Amends can range from apologies to actual acts that involve use of our time and treasures. Thistle Farms has been the recipient of several anonymous gifts over the years given by people who were making amends for some of their past mistakes. All the money was used to directly help women find sanctuary. In your prayer and reflection, ask yourself what might be an appropriate way to demonstrate your desire to make things right.

4. Move On

It's good to remember your mistakes enough to let them humble you sufficiently. But do not allow them to shame you or make you think you are alone or that you may never get better. Love is stronger than anything you have done. The greater mistake would be to let your past deeds cripple you.

An old saying goes something like this: the difference between a saint and a sinner is that the sinner falls six times, but the saint falls six times and gets up seven. No matter how far we have fallen, God's love can help us rise again. In the fourteenth century, theologian Julian of Norwich said, "It is true that sin is the cause of all this suffering, but all shall be well, and all shall be well, and all manner of things shall be well." That sentiment still echoes through prison walls, through rocky trails where we stumble, through tight circles of disciples, and through the lavish pouring out of all our shame and fear. We shall be well.

A Prayer of Faithfulness

Prepare me, dear Lord, to start this day again.
I am ready to keep climbing even though the mountain is steep.
I am willing to keep searching even though the fog is thick.
I am able to keep praying even though my words sound hollow.
Take these offerings, and use them to open my heart to a new
    song.
Remove from me all that is keeping me unwilling or unable to sing
    so that I can praise the wonder of clouds parting and Love
    revealed. Amen.

No matter how far
we have fallen,
God's love can help
us rise up again.

CHAPTER 12

LOVE HEALS OVER THE BRIDGE OF TIME

Making space to let healing happen

Original Love

Before a path was chosen

Or a word spoken,

Before a wall was built

Or an apple bitten,

Before people were dressed

Or a prayer was offered,

Before a sword was forged

Or the seas parted,

Before a war was fought

Or a winter passed,

Before the wine was blessed

Or bread was broken,

There was love.

ealing takes time. Since we can't control time, the best we can do is create a safe environment where healing can be explored. Creating that environment is an ongoing endeavor that takes a persistent faith.

The Gospels tell the beautiful story of the persistent widow. In Luke's parable, the woman has to plead with a judge who doesn't fear God or even care about justice, but because the widow bothers him day and night with her pleas, he grants her justice. Jesus said to the disciples, "Will not God bring about justice for his chosen ones, who cry out to him day and night?" (Luke 18:7).

We are called to be persistent in our pursuit of healing. Yet there is a point, as there is in exercise, recovery, and parenting, where we hit plateaus. We aren't seeing much improvement or change, and so we want to give up. But time and persistence keep working even when we can't see any visible change.

We have to trust that healing is happening and keep practicing what we know we are supposed to do. Then healing will unfold in new and unimagined ways. We will be so grateful we didn't give up.

My sister, Sandy, who is a doctor, got her first degree in occupational therapy. She went on a teaching mission to Cameroon in Africa, and while she was teaching, she was in a horrible bus crash in which five people died. After being medically evacuated to Switzerland and undergoing several surgeries, she ended up losing her pinkie finger and a small part of her hand. I flew to Switzerland to be with her and watched her struggle with pain and her inability to use both of her arms during the healing process. She couldn't shampoo her hair or brush her teeth. She came home and spent months rehabilitating and working on getting strength and mobility back. In the first months, her hands were so immobile and shaky that she couldn't even hold coins. I admired how she never despaired and how, even with scars running all the way down both arms, she was committed to healing so she could help others.

The next year, my oldest son, Levi, cut his hand on a broken window. He went to a hand surgeon, who said he would need a good occupational therapist to work with his pinkie finger because the tendons and nerves on his hand were severed—at the very same place that was cut on my sister's hand. I told the doctor I knew the best healer for him, and Levi started seeing my sister, Sandy, for hand therapy. She didn't have that part of her own body, but through time and love and patience, she made Levi feel hopeful and safe.

As I watched them work together night after night, I kept thinking about all those months she spent working on her own healing and how through that long work she had been getting strong enough to help my son heal. He was scared about so many things, but having his aunt, who had gone through even more and who was unending in her devotion to his healing, helped him over those months. Time and safety are truly some of the greatest gifts we can find when we are searching for healing. Persistence is the key and time is the means by which healing unfolds.

Persistence is the key
and time is the means by
which healing unfolds.

A Safe Place for Time to Do Its Healing Work

It's important for all of us to find a safe environment where we can discover the healing possible in our lives—where we can let time pass and do its work. Sometimes in the thick of crises, grief, and pain, it's hard to get a perspective on how healing can come. Time offers that perspective. Time itself doesn't do the healing, but using all the tools we've explored over time can. It just takes persistence, strength, and hope.

I have borne witness to hundreds of stories of crises when women came off the streets or out of prison. Sometimes the women looked like they were beyond healing, or it seemed their lives were such a mess that there was no way out. But that is why we offer a two-year time period for women to live in the Thistle Farms community and focus on healing—for change to take root. Sometimes healing is so slow that you can't even tell anything is happening. But then, over months, as the women are working and seeing their kids and they begin to make restitution with courts and credit records—a light dawns in their eyes.

One woman came into the program because she believed she was dying. There was almost nothing left of her, and her disease had left her mother planning a funeral and preparing to raise her child. Yet after a year or so, she became one of the strongest leaders in the community. Over that year we reminded her that this way of living wasn't a dream and that her old life was behind her. She would be well. Ten years later, she still weeps when talking about what love did to bring her back. She will never forget how hard it was and how long it took for the miracle to happen.

Eventually this woman married and built a house. And then her mom died. Her mother had been her rock and stronghold, and she did not think she could get over that loss. Again, she relied on the safety of her community and trusted that time would help. More than three years have passed since then, and while she still misses her mom, she has healed from deep, paralyzing grief.

We don't have to know how long healing will take; we just have to keep praying and working like the widow before the judge. Time opens up room for healing to take root in us.

Finding a safe place for the healing work of time is unique to everyone. For some it will be a church community; for others it will be the sanctuary of the woods. Still others find safety in their homes, in recovery rooms, or in the presence of someone they called beloved. It is where the word *home* fits and where peace dwells.

Walk, Don't Run

Minds, bodies, and hearts do not heal at the same rate. Scars can heal over on our bodies while the emotional trauma is still alive and kicking. As we are developing skills to cope with traumas of our past, we need to be gentle with ourselves and others. Part of coping means *we* have to change and relearn what it is we thought we already knew. None of this happens overnight. But love starts to whisper every now and then in our ears that we are stronger than the memories and scars. Even when a bone heals, we have to be gentle with that part of ourselves for months afterward—we keep it protected and make sure no one runs into it. Almost always, healing is a walk, not a run. The same is true for the deeper wounds in our hearts. We keep our hearts protected so they can grow strong. It takes time after a break-up or trauma to be healthy enough to be in a loving relationship again.

Another way I've learned how love heals over time comes from the lessons of parenting. Parenting has given me a new perspective on time and how it helps us heal and grow. In child rearing, I think it's fair to say that years fly by and afternoons tick away slowly. I can't see it, but my children are growing into their full stature right before my eyes. I have now watched all three of my sons grow taller than me. It is a wonder of time that I never could have imagined when they came into this world. Scripture reminds us of this by calling out one key thing: "With the Lord a day is like a thousand years, and a thousand years are like a day" (2 Peter 3:8). All the time we are given as parents is a reminder that love heals and grows that which is most precious in our lives.

Time, as a teacher, asks us to remember simply to create safe places, to walk and not run in this work, and to enjoy the gift of time as healing takes place. If we can remember those three things, we will be as patient as Job and as faithful as Simeon who sang after years of sitting in the temple:

"Lord, you now have set your servant free to go in peace as you have promised;

For these eyes of mine have seen the Savior, whom you have prepared for all the world to see."

—Luke 2:29–31, Book of Common Prayer

CHAPTER 13

LOVE HEALS BEYOND STRESS

*Learning to cope and
lessen anxiety*

Dancing with Cicadas

The cicada's high-pitched,

Wavy, tymbal song commences.

It feels like stress incarnate in sound.

It builds from white noise

Into the forefront of thought,

Pushing peace to the recesses of memory.

The woods buzz like a loud club,

Where noise rises beyond reason.

People are drowned out of thought.

It sounds like techno music

Suddenly calling us to the dance floor,

Translucent disco wings beating.

The pulsing sound shifts from stressful

To delight with dervish drumming.

I hope they don't quiet down until

I feel dizzy from this dancing.

The cicada is not made to stress

But to help us find rhythm and dance.

Stress can kill. Slowly but surely it tightens our chests, increases our heart rates, causes our stomachs to ache, stiffens our necks, and manifests itself a million other ways within our bodies. The effects of stress have been studied on children, prisoners, people in power, parents, and throughout various socioeconomic classes. In a study reported by CBS in 2003, researchers demonstrated how chronic stress can actually kill people. No one is immune to stress, but we can learn to manage it by developing daily coping skills and setting long-term paths that will offer us freedom. While we wait for time to do its healing work, dealing with stress means seeing the details right before us *and* the bigger picture, both of which lead us to healing.

It is a misconception that the stress we feel today is because of the current pace of life, the spread of technology, or the political turmoil we see around us and throughout the world. A great English theologian of the nineteenth century, Frederick D. Morris, wrote about the dis-ease of busyness and how it causes stress, a depleted spirituality, and decline within the ranks of the church. He wrote that the busyness that causes harm to us comes from our distrust of God. We search frantically for things to give us peace, but the search leaves us restless. Morris was not saying that we can't be busy; he was saying that we need to be busy with things that matter in this world. When we make our busyness the focus of our life and worth, we become stressed, restless, and unhealthy.

When we learn how to manage the demands on our lives and cope with

I know that if I
make time for God,
God will make time
for everything else.

the worries of the day, we are putting our faith in into practice and we are healthier for it. Years ago, when I was first starting out in this work of healing at Thistle Farms, I met a woman who had eleven children. She said she started every day by going to mass at a nearby church. I asked her how, with all the demands and the stress of that number of children, did she make time for that? Her answer was simple: "I know that if I make time for God, God will make time for everything else."

She was not stressed, and the peace emanating from her heart taught me a great lesson to carry into my work and motherhood. We will always be busy, but if we have our eyes on the long-term goal of being faithful and the short-term goal of making time for God, everything else will fall into place.

Long-Term Faithfulness

Jesus taught the disciples how to manage stress with His beautiful call: "Do not worry." At the beginning of their journey to Jerusalem, the disciples had many reasons to stress. The crowds were pressing in, the religious authorities were bearing down, they had left everything, and the occupied nation was struggling with violence and oppression. In the midst of all of this, Jesus stopped and asked them this simple question: "Can any one of you by worrying add a single hour to your life?" (Matthew 6:27). When Jesus uses the word *worry*, I think of it as another word for *stress*.

When we worry about our lives, about what the day holds, or if we will be okay, we become distracted and stressed and lose our way. Jesus reminds us that in the midst of all the busyness, suffering, and fear, we do not have to worry. Our loving God gives us all we need. God promises that our lives will have meaning and we will live forever. There is no better assurance to relieve our stress.

Short-Term Practices

People try to give you their stress, sometimes without even knowing it. You can be driving down a street, sitting at a desk, or grocery shopping, and someone may come up to you and, with just a few words or even a look, fill you with stress. We are stressed by things that haven't even happened yet. We worry over things we cannot change. In order to live on a healing path, we need to develop good medicine to keep our worries and stress in check. I have seen healing power in these seven basic practices that can help us cope with both daily and long-term stress.

1. Pray Daily

As the mother of eleven did, begin the day with a focus on faith. It keeps at bay all the small stresses that rob our joy and the big worries that keep us depressed.

The Lord taught us this daily prayer to keep our focus where it should be (translation from the Book of Common Prayer © 1979):

> Our Father, who art in heaven, hallowed be thy name.
> Thy kingdom come, thy will be done, on earth as it is in
> heaven.
> Give us this day, our daily bread, and forgive us our
> trespasses,
> As we forgive those who trespass against us.
> And lead us not into temptation, but deliver us from evil,
> For thine is the kingdom, the power and the glory,
> Now and forever. Amen.
>
> MATTHEW 6:9–13

2. Create Free Time

In the context of stress management, the definition of *free time* is time you choose to use however you wish. Your free time is something you must cultivate and protect. It can't be bought and it can't be imposed. It is simply a gift in your day that you accept. It can be used for thinking, advocating, goofing off, volunteering, napping, writing, exercising, or even cleaning. The most important thing is that you give yourself freedom for a time so you can do whatever your heart desires.

3. Develop Healthy Sleep Rituals

How you prepare for bed, how you create your sleeping space, and how long you give yourself to rest can determine your ability to manage stress in your waking hours. Let a prayer of gratitude be your final thought as you surrender the day, your family, and your future into the loving arms of your Lord. Turn off the TV, feel safe under the covers, and let yourself feel your heart slowing and breath deepening so you can truly rest in peace.

4. Daydream

Daydreaming is a skill that allows you to feel inspired by new thoughts, takes you away from mundane tasks that can make you feel depressed, and can even carry you back to times when you felt the peace of a mountain-top or the restfulness of the beach. When you daydream, you are allowing yourself the space to follow thoughts to their conclusions and see if there is peace in their wake. Then you can either develop that thought or let it go. Daydreaming has allowed artists to paint and writers to find muses. Daydreaming reduces stress and gives us glimpses of new possibilities.

5. Keep a Student's Heart

Never stop learning, reading, and listening. So often, people guard their positions or intellectual territory like bulldogs. It is stressful to stay in that mode. But when you make yourself open to new people and new ideas, some of the old stresses disappear as you quit feeling like you have to defend everything. When you continue learning and studying (without being graded on the final!), you learn to maintain a calmer heart. And any mistakes you make, you can chalk up to a life lesson.

6. Understand Pain as a Teacher

This is a difficult truth to practice in the moment of crisis. But pain has so much to teach us. It can teach us when we need to slow down or rest, when we need to do things differently, when we need to ask for help, and when we need to get tough and bear through it. Pain gives us hard lessons, but when we can see it as a teacher, it can show us what we need to change and help us find the way to relief and healing.

7. Laugh!

We don't need to take everything so seriously—especially ourselves. At Thistle Farms we meet each other in a "daily circle" every morning, and I love that in this gathering we laugh as much as we cry. Even in the midst of stress, when we can find humor in our lives, we have made a giant stride toward healing. One of my favorite teachers on this is Dorris, a great survivor-leader who can have us all in stitches as she describes her first visit to a doctor, or the time her wig fell off at a store, or even in stories about her last days on the streets. She speaks with great wisdom laced with just the right amount of humor—and you can see the healing at work as her words bring us to tears of laughter.

Working through stress helps us discover peaceful places where we feel hopeful about what tomorrow will bring. It assures us that love is healing us every day. Remember that if you stress because you feel like your glass is half empty most of the time, your cup may be too big. Speak kindly to others. Count your blessings every day. Build your faith in the long and short term. Love heals beyond the stress and calls us to make time for God and find His peace.

> LORD, my heart is not haughty,
> Nor my eyes lofty.
> Neither do I concern myself with great matters,
> Nor with things too profound for me.
> Surely I have calmed and quieted my soul,
> Like a weaned child with his mother;
> Like a weaned child is my soul within me.
> O Israel, hope in the LORD
> From this time forth and forever.
>
> PSALM 131 NKJV

If you stress because you feel like your glass is half empty most of the time, your cup may be too big.

CHAPTER 14

LOVE HEALS PAST OUR FEARS

Walking through anxiety

Night Fears

From here there is no night sky.
Birds are silent in distant trees.
Without a star I can't wish or find north.
Old ghosts who wish me harm visit.
I am melting into it as fear
Squeezes against my chest,
Calling me into oblivion.
If I am allowed one prayer,
Even if I don't believe a word of it,
As my throat clenches,
I pray the dawn is coming,
And in the gray light,
I will hear a bird sing.
I will endure this night
Filled with things known and unknown,
Trusting the morning star will rise,
And love will push fear aside.

Fear keeps a troubled vigil at night and wraps our brightest days in a shroud. It is hard to accept the harsh events of this world that leave us vulnerable and afraid. Sometimes we succumb to that fear-filled place inside. Being afraid is normal, and like pain, fear can be a hard but valuable teacher on our path to healing. Of all the obstacles to healing we have discussed, fear can outweigh all the others. Of all the lessons I have learned from the community of Thistle Farms, the greatest is to work and pray past my fears. The courage and faith it takes to work past fears offers the rewards of new life, inspiration, and hope. To me, this is the culmination of how love heals. We remove barrier after barrier and feel the great healing power of love.

I have hiked on wooded trails for years. I have felt fear rise as something unseen shakes the bushes. My pulse races, I jump, and I know that the primordial-fear instinct is alive and well! Sometimes I have been startled by an unfamiliar rustle, and that reflex has saved me. Once, while walking through the Tennessee hills in the heat of summer, I almost stepped on a big rattlesnake. I heard it at the last second as my fear enabled me—on a dime—to stop dead in my tracks as the fat, coiled-up viper shook his tail and stuck out his tongue in my direction. Slowly I was able to walk backward until I felt safe. As fear left me, I felt shaky and wanted to laugh. That kind of fear is useful and protects us from things that can do us harm.

There are fears, though, that can stifle us—fears that keep us trapped in a comfort zone that doesn't expand our wisdom, our ability to love, or our understanding of the world. Those fears live in all of us, and they keep us separated from love. To find God's healing truth, we must recognize when our fears are stumbling blocks. In seminary I was taught that fear is the opposite of love. So when I am able to step over the stumbling blocks of fear, I am closer to finding love. That lesson, however, also falls into the category of "easier said than done." When we first opened Thistle Farms, I remember walking down some of the most dangerous streets in Nashville to reach out to some of the women I wanted to serve. I felt real fear, but I knew that I needed to do this work in order to be faithful to my calling. I found that gathering a community diminished the fear, and that I could walk with fear alongside me.

Follow or Flee?

Fear can be both protective and problematic. We learn from Proverbs that "the fear of the LORD is the beginning of wisdom" (9:10). That is a healthy fear that puts us in right relationship and shows us how fear can be used to our benefit. But the angels in the Bible often told the people of Israel, "Fear not." So it seems the path to healing is about discerning which fear to embrace and which fear to flee.

As we seek healing, we are called to follow our fear, because past that fear lies all the other aspects of healing we are seeking—freedom, mercy, and even joy. When we bump into fear, we can use it as a signal that this is a good place to stop and take stock. So the next time you feel fear rising in your throat, ask yourself, *What am I really afraid of? Am I getting ready to step on a snake, or am I scared to grow deeper into faith and be free? Will this fear stop me from learning something new? Will it close a door that I need to walk through? Will it hurt someone else?* Such moments are climatic, and they point to all the lessons we have discussed in this book. They are moments when we think about our pasts, our grief, our need to forgive, and our daily practices.

When we discern that the fear before us is a stumbling block, trying to move past it can feel undoable. Personally, I can't will myself to overcome fear, pretend I am making peace with it, or "let it go." I don't take comfort in the words "This too shall pass" or "We shall overcome." I just feel scared. That doesn't mean I stop trying. It means I need to keep trying. I need to keep fear from having the last word on how I live. For example, if you are afraid to fly, it doesn't mean you stop flying. It means that you need to figure out *how* to fly. Are there things you can do to ease your anxiety? Are there people who can help you? Are there others who have overcome this who can teach you?

Fear is cunning—it can crop up on us in the middle of the night or visit in our weakest place and time. And we can't avoid it. But we can treat our fears with compassion, trust that we can either overcome or learn from them, and respect their power in our daily lives. Learning to live with our fears and doing things beyond our fears requires us to be brave on our healing path.

Living with Fear

Several women from Thistle Farms have been in and out of prison most of their lives. They talk about the fear of being arrested—and the fear of being released. That fear is always lurking in the shadows during times of crisis and stress. One woman said that she was always in prison whether or not she was in jail because she lived in fear: fear of the violence, sickness, and dangers on the streets. She said that sometimes she feared being out of prison more than being behind bars. "In there," she said, "I never get raped or beaten, and I can sleep. Out here, I don't know if I will make it through the night." The entire first six months she was at Thistle Farms, she felt fear—not because anything bad was going to happen but because so much bad *had* happened. Her fears would not let her believe she could live differently.

As this woman became more trusting with time and with tools to live, she became less fearful, inspiring all of us to be brave and learn to live with fear until love moves it aside. She said it helped to stay busy, to have friends, and to develop the skills to see into fear so she could see the difference between fear keeping her from stepping on a snake and fear that is

How do we discern if our fear is good or a stumbling block? Ask a simple question: "Is this fear potentially enhancing my quality of life or stifling me?"

just a stumbling block in her way. Her story teaches us that we can't avoid fear, and we can't will it to go away. Instead we keep going, even as we fear. When we follow our fears on the healing path, love eventually moves our fears aside.

Beyond Our Fear

Only as we truly engage our fears do we learn the power of love. We may never completely overcome our fears. Great heroes have felt fear as much as those of us who have cowered in the shadows. What makes someone heroic is their ability to recognize fear and to trust in something stronger than the fear. Love doesn't abandon us in our fears. God tells us: "Do not fear, for I am with you; do not be dismayed, for I am your God. I will strengthen you and help you; I will uphold you with my righteous right hand" (Isaiah 41:10).

Of all the lessons I have learned, recognizing and discerning my fears has been one of the greatest. Fear doesn't trip me up; I am ready to meet fear. My fears have taught me what it means to need others, how to listen as I sit by the bedsides of the dying, and that the old ghosts from my past have no power over me. As a young entrepreneur and pastor, I harbored so many fears. I was scared we wouldn't meet payroll, that a woman who had relapsed would be killed, or that I wasn't generous enough or—maybe worse—capable enough. These fears were powerful and kept my dreams small and my anxiety high. This book is an explanation of how living into my faith more than my fears has been healing to me personally and healing for the community. The payrolls were always met, none of the relapses killed the program or hope, and when I wasn't enough, others stepped in and led. Fear still creeps up, and there are still restless nights, but now a beautiful community stands tall and powerful against those fears. It is healing to discover that fear doesn't get the last word or decide our future.

Fear is one of the biggest obstacles in healing, and so it may be our greatest teacher. When I was flying with a new resident of Magdalene recently, she leaned across me as she gazed intently at the night sky and haloed full moon. There was a blanket of back-lit clouds below. Because she had been on the streets since seventh grade, she knew precious little about the world. It was magnificent. She looked up at me and said that she had never considered how there was sky above the clouds. She told me that seeing the heavens at night took the fear of the night she had held for so long and cast it aside. I admired her so much for saying that she had been afraid and that she was feeling the joy of that fear being set aside. Whenever she gets afraid from now on, she will have that vision of the world opening up to her and how she saw the glory of God's creation and felt healed.

On Love's healing path, fear will always move out of the way, because always, Love is more powerful than fear.

Love, as we have seen throughout this book, moves mountains, it sits by us daily, it is filled with mercy and compassion, and it reaches across the world and through time. Love expands our hearts, it sits still with us, it grieves with us, and it heals us. Love gives us a glimpse of the glorious heavens and the fearful valley. Love gives us ears to hear the angel say once again to us, "Fear not, for God is with you."

A Prayer in Times of Fear

God, we make our prayer in silence, troubled by the fears in our hearts and anxieties in this world. Forgive all that we have yet to learn and when we feel panic and are tortured by insecurity. We can be paralyzed by the thought of tomorrow and what awaits in the days ahead. We are but children stumbling in the darkness and groping for Your hand. Do not hide Your presence from us or reject us in our weaknesses and fear. Guide us in the darkness toward Your loving light, and help us walk in peace. There are so many things to fear and so many fears that keep us lonely. Let us put our whole trust in You and come to wisdom and understanding—and all for love's sake. Amen.

ABOUT THISTLE FARMS

Since our beginnings, Thistle Farms has offered sanctuary with the mission to be a witness to the truth that, in the end, love is the most powerful force for change in the world. Ever since the first five women came to live at Magdalene (now called Thistle Farms) in 1997, our goals were clear: to create community, not clients; to help change a culture that still bought and sold women as commodities; and to create homes, not halfway houses or shelters. Over the past twenty years, we've been amazed at how God has used this environment to bring healing to women who suffer from wounds and scars that seem incurable.

The residential community of Thistle Farms offers two years of free housing with no authority in the homes—meaning that the women are not supervised but live with independence. The residential arm of Thistle

Farms provides medical care, therapy, education, and job training without charging residents or receiving government funding. Our hope is for the entire community to give to one another in gratitude for all the mercy and healing we have known. The women work to gain financial independence through the social enterprises of Thistle Farms, which produces candles and body-care products and operates a café and artisan studio under the motto, of course, *Love heals*. It reminds everyone who uses the products that, deeper than all the scars women carry from childhood trauma, rape, and whatever pain befalls them, there is healing.

We wanted to make products that were healing for the earth and our bodies and that would offer healing to all the people in the world whom we still called strangers. In 2014, in response to the universal issues of trafficking and addiction, we started a national alliance of sister programs across the country and a global initiative called "Shared Trade" to link women survivors around the world through a common distribution system and community support. We have always tried to grow and expand where love leads us. We have opened up sewing cooperatives, paper studios, and tea companies in response to the needs of women trying to heal from some of the deepest scars this world has to offer. We are still growing and healing to this day.

There is no secret to our success. Our business is an open book that supports volunteers and thousands of annual visitors to the company, where people tour the facility and can drink a healing cup of thistle tea at the Thistle Stop Café in Nashville, Tennessee. Each day we deal with these businesses, we find that love is an endless commodity we can tap into when we put people first and swear we won't leave any sisters behind. Over all the years and the travel I have done, I have come to believe that if you want to kill a village, rape the women. If you want to heal a village, heal the women. The women of Thistle Farms are bringing healing and practical ideas to create sanctuary to cities across the United States. We are speaking at hundreds of churches, conventions, and gatherings to spread the truth of how love is lavish and economical. Just by our presence in Nashville, Tennessee, we bring over three-quarters of a million dollars in savings and revenues to the city. We are part of a wider movement that is changing the tide of the conversation away from blame and shame and toward practical healing with quantifiable value.

We will continue to rise to the occasion for the thousands of women still on the streets—who deserve to be more than just survivors of child rape, trafficking, prostitution, and addiction. One of the residential graduates says the biggest lie she was told when she was sold to a drug dealer as a teenager was that she was stupid. But as she and all her sisters work, heal, and grow through Thistle Farms, they are proving every day that they are more than what they were led to believe and that their potential is unimaginable.

Today the residential program of Thistle Farms serves more than seven hundred women yearly with advocacy and referral services, as well as managing our two-year residential program and an inmate program. Residents, staff, and our entire community are guided by *twenty-four spiritual principles*:

1. Come Together
2. Proclaim Original Grace
3. Cry with Your Creator
4. Find Your Place in the Circle
5. Think of the Stranger as God
6. Take the Longer Path
7. Make a Small Change
8. Let God Sort It Out
9. Stand on New Ground
10. Forgive and Feel Freedom
11. Unite Your Sexuality and Spirituality
12. Show Hospitality to All
13. Laugh at Yourself
14. Consider the Thistle
15. Listen to a New Idea
16. Lose Gracefully
17. Remember You Have Been in the Ditch
18. Walk Behind
19. Live in Gratitude

20. Love Without Judgment
21. Stay on Point
22. Pray for Courage
23. Find Your Way Home
24. Leave Thankfully

Thistle Farms is not done expanding or dreaming. Groups in other cities are looking to us to help them open new residences. We want to reach out to other global communities with refugees displaced by war and poverty and all the injustices and violence that spring from such brutality, because they need to find distribution for their handmade products and access to better services for women surviving trauma. There are more jobs with better wages to be created and a deep need for more sanctuary and healing. We are just beginning to hit our stride for the journey ahead.

Through the witness of the first women who came to find sanctuary with us, to the thousands who have now become thriving members of our community through work and partnerships that are living testimonies to the healing power of love, I have learned that God's love is unstoppable. As you find your own healing, I invite you to visit us online or in person and be encouraged on your healing path by those receiving new life in beautiful and exciting ways every day at Thistle Farms.

www.thistlefarms.org

ABOUT THE AUTHOR

Becca Stevens is an author, speaker, social entrepreneur, and founder and president of Thistle Farms, the largest social enterprise in the United States run by survivors. An international voice for the global movement for women's freedom and a defender of the marginalized, she has been named a "Champion of Change" by the White House for her work against domestic violence, "Humanitarian of the Year" by a number of organizations, and a "2016 CNN Hero." Becca has received two honorary doctorates and lives in Nashville, Tennessee, where she serves as an Episcopal priest and lives with her Grammy-winning songwriter husband and three sons.

Love is the most powerful force for healing.